Timothy Shay Arthur

Anna Lee: The Maiden, the Wife and the Mother

Timothy Shay Arthur

Anna Lee: The Maiden, the Wife and the Mother

ISBN/EAN: 9783337023690

Printed in Europe, USA, Canada, Australia, Japan

Cover: Foto ©ninafisch / pixelio.de

More available books at **www.hansebooks.com**

THE MOTHER.
Page 182.

ANNA LEE:

THE MAIDEN—THE WIFE—THE MOTHER.

A Tale.

BY

T. S. ARTHUR,

AUTHOR OF "TRUE RICHES; OR, WEALTH WITHOUT WINGS,"
ETC. ETC.

'Maid, wife, and mother; each succeeding tie
That Love reveals from out his hidden stores,
Bringing to light fresh springs, that joyously
Well forth with richest fulness, as each pours
Its wealth of treasures,—found alone complete
Where love out-pours them, at a mother's feet."

LONDON:
T. NELSON AND SONS, PATERNOSTER ROW;
EDINBURGH; AND NEW YORK.
1876.

CONTENTS

THE MAIDEN.

Chap.		Page
I.	Duty before Pleasure,	9
II.	Gardiner's True Character exhibited,	21
III.	The Beauty and Power of Goodness,	24
IV.	True Maiden Delicacy and its Opposite contrasted,	27
V.	The Maiden's First Strong Trial,	31
VI.	Tried and Proved,	38
VII.	A Disappointment,	45
VIII.	A Wise Selection of Friends,	49
IX.	Catching Husbands,	51
X.	A New Lover,	55
XI.	An Impression made,	60
XII.	Wooed and Won,	63
XIII.	Conclusion,	69

THE WIFE.

I.	An Effort to begin right—A Wise Decision,	73
II.	A Thoughtless Woman of the World—Florence Armitage,	81
III.	A Slight Misunderstanding,	91
IV.	All Right Again,	100
V.	House Furnishing,	107
VI.	A Prudent Course the Wisest,	113
VII.	A Foolish Wife,	118
VIII.	A Sad Picture of Domestic Life,	126
IX.	False Friends,	134
X.	Marriage changes Social Relations,	140
XI.	Mrs. Riston's House-warming,	144
XII.	How it affected her Husband's Credit,	152
XIII.	Taking a Lower Place in Society,	162
XIV.	True Love tried and proved,	166
XV.	A Change,	176
XVI.	Conclusion	181

THE MOTHER.

Chap.		Page
I.	Introduction,	185
II.	Beginning Right,	192
III.	Means and Ends,	196
IV.	The Secret of Governing Children,	198
V.	A Mother's Influence,	201
VI.	Correcting a Fault,	216
VII.	Strong Contrast,	223
VIII.	More Contrasts,	231
IX.	Fruit,	238
X.	An Agreeable Surprise,	247
XI.	Going into Company,	254
XII.	A Painful Bereavement,	261
XIII.	An Important Era in Life,	270
XIV.	Happy Consummations,	273
XV.	Conclusion,	277

ANNA LEE:

THE MAIDEN—THE WIFE—THE MOTHER.

The Maiden.

CHAPTER I.

DUTY BEFORE PLEASURE.

"ANNA, dear," said Mrs. Lee in a quiet tone to her eldest daughter, a young maiden over whose head the blossoms of only eighteen happy summers had fallen, "it is time you were beginning to dress for the party at Mrs. Leslie's."

Anna Lee sat sewing near a window, and was bending closer towards the light, as it was beginning gradually to withdraw before the shadows of an autumn evening. She let the work fall into her lap, and mused for a short time. Then turning her soft blue eyes upon her mother, she said,—

"I believe I won't go this evening."

"Why not, Anna? You have made every preparation. What has caused you to change your mind?"

The maiden sat again silent for nearly a minute, evidently debating whether she should go out or not. Company had been invited at the house of an acquaintance, where she had fully intended to spend the evening.

"I don't think I ought to go," she replied, a little evasively.

"Why, dear?"

"I think I shall be happier at home, mother."

"But we should not always consult our own feelings. Think whether your absence will not take from the pleasure of some of Mrs. Leslie's guests. Some of your young friends will miss you. I think I would go, Anna; if not for my own sake, for the sake of others."

"And may I not stay at home for the same reason?" said Anna, going quickly to the side of her mother, who sat in a large chair, her face pale and wearing an expression of languor. She drew her arm around her mother's neck as she spoke.

"You may, if such a reason can keep you at home," replied Mrs. Lee.

"I think it does require me to stay at home. You are not so well to-day, and I cannot bear to have you worried with giving the children their suppers and putting them to bed. John and Charlie are rude to Margaret, and never will let her do anything for them without a disturbance. Your head has ached dreadfully, and has only been easy for the last hour. If you should have to see after the children, the pain will come back, and then you will get no rest all night."

Mrs. Lee did not immediately reply. Her feelings were touched at the affectionate, self-sacrificing spirit of her child. But she could not bear the thought of having her forego the enjoyment of a social evening on her account.

"I think, Anna," she at length said, "that I am a great deal better, and that it will not hurt me in the least to see after the children. So don't think anything more about me, but go and get yourself ready at once."

Anna stood in an attitude and with an expression of irresolution upon her countenance.

"Go, dear," urged the mother; "I wish you to do so."

"I'll go and see after the children first."

And Anna passed with light steps from the room.

"Dear, good girl!" murmured the mother, sinking languidly back in her chair, as her daughter vanished from her sight.

Anna went to the dining-room, where four children were romping and making a loud noise—some singing at the top of their voices, and others pounding on the floor, and dragging about the chairs. Among them was a little girl named Mary, four years old, who was dancing and singing as loud as the rest. As Anna came in, she became quiet, drew up to her side, and took fast hold of her hand.

"John," said Anna, speaking in a mild, yet firm voice, to the eldest boy, who was hammering on the floor, "mother is not well this evening. Your noise will make her head ache."

John looked up at his sister a moment, but did not heed her words. He continued to make as much noise as before.

"I've a beautiful story to tell you all," the elder sister now said.

This had the effect she desired. John threw down his hammer, Charlie let go the chair he was dragging around the room, and all of them gathered quietly around their sister, and looked up eagerly into her face.

Anna told them a touching little story about some children whose mother took sick and died, and left them to be taken care of by strangers, who were not kind to them as their own dear mother had been. Tears were in the eyes of two of the children; but John, though interested, seemed but little affected by the narrative.

"Tell us another story, sister," said Mary.

"Yes, sister, do," urged the other children.

And Anna told them another story.

"Now, another."

"I've told you two good stories. And now I must get you all your suppers."

"You're not going to get my supper," said John, in an ill-natured tone. "I shall eat with father and mother."

"And so shall I," responded Charlie.

"Oh, no," mildly returned Anna. "Mother has been sick to-day; so you must all eat your suppers together, and go quietly to bed. Your noise disturbs her."

"To bed, indeed! Ho! ho! I'm not going to bed these two hours yet."

"O yes, John, you are. If mother is sick, and wants you to go to bed early, I am sure you will go."

"I'm going to sit up. If mother is sick, my sitting up won't hurt her. I've got all my lessons to learn."

"You can study them in the morning just as well, and a great deal better. So, John, be a good boy, and eat your supper with the other children."

"No, I won't—so there now, Miss! And you need not say another word about it."

Anna sighed as she turned away from her brother, whose natural disposition was showing its inherent evil tendencies so early, and began to prepare the children's supper. When it was ready, she lifted the two younger children, Jane and Mary, into their places, and then turning to Charlie, she stooped over him, and whispered something in his ear.

The boy instantly took his place at the table, with a smile upon his face. But John was not to be moved. He resolutely persisted in refusing to eat his supper then.

After Anna had helped all the little ones at the table, she went to where John was sitting in a chair, in a sulky mood; and taking a seat beside him, said, in a calm, mild voice,—

"John, mother has not been well all day. She has suffered very much with headache, and is only now a little better. I want to go out this evening, but can't begin to get ready until I have given you all your suppers, and seen you to bed. Won't you then, for my sake, eat with the other children now, and then go to bed like a good boy?"

"No, I will not!" This was said very ill-naturedly.

"O yes, John, I am sure you will."

"But I tell you I won't. I'm not going off to bed just because you wish me to do so. Go, if you will, but don't trouble yourself about me. I'll eat my supper when father comes home."

Anna was grieved, as she often before had been, at John's unkindness and self-will. And she even felt a rising emotion of anger; but this she quickly suppressed. Turning from him, she waited upon her brother and sisters who were at the table, and when they were done, took them up into their chamber, and laid them all snugly in their beds; not, however, before telling them several stories, and hearing them say in turn a little prayer. Kissing each sweet face, she took the lamp, and descended to the dining-room. It was nearly an hour since she left her mother in her own chamber. She found John still fixed in his resolution to sit up, as he was in the habit of doing. After one or two efforts to dissuade him from his purpose, she left him alone, and went into her mother's room. It was still an hour before Mr. Lee was expected home.

"Why, Anna, dear, why are you not getting ready to go to Mrs. Leslie's?"

"I've just got the children, all but John, off to bed. He wants to sit up and eat with you and father."

"Well, let him. He can go to bed himself when he gets sleepy. So now, make haste and put on your things."

Anna went out, and ascended to her own chamber; but she was little inclined to do as her mother had urged her. The effort she had made to induce John to do as she wished him, and his unkind return, had depressed her spirits, and caused her to feel disinclined to go into company. But this she conquered in a little while, and recollecting that she was to be called for at seven, she commenced making the necessary preparations. While engaged in laying out and arranging the clothes she intended wearing, loud and angry words were heard by her from the kitchen, between John and the cook. Descending quickly, in order to check the disturbance before it should reach the ears of her mother, she found that the perverse boy had been endeavouring to interfere with some of the cook's operations. That individual justly opposed him, and this produced a contention between them, the result of which was a blow over John's head with the tongs, well laid on, just at the moment of Anna's entrance. John was seizing the shovel, when his sister caught his arm. Feeling that he had been in the wrong, and checked by Anna's presence, he let the weapon fall, though not without an angrily uttered threat of what he would do to the cook.

Anna now decided that she would not go out. If her mother had been well, she would easily have managed John. But Anna knew, from the excited state of her nerves, that if she were compelled to leave her room to check such a scene, it would bring back upon her the dreadful headache and sick stomach from which she had all day been suffering.

"It will be wrong for me to leave her, and I will not do so," she said to herself, resolutely.

The person who was to call for Anna, and accompany her to the party, was a young man named Herbert Gardiner. The fair young face and sweet temper of

Anna Lee had won upon his feelings; and, in consequence, he had thrown himself into her company whenever he could do so. As for Anna, all unconfessed to herself, her heart had begun to feel an interest in the young man. The fact that he was to call for her was a strong inducement; but a sense of duty was a much stronger feeling, and she suffered it, as has been seen, to prevail.

Such a state of mind, so far in advance of most young persons, was not a mere natural growth—was not the regular maturity of germs of good, hereditarily derived—it was the result of sound maternal precepts, and a most earnest care that the tender mind of her child, in its development, should be moulded into a right form. Early had Mrs. Lee taught her first-born the highest and best lesson a human being can learn —to imitate God in seeking to bless others. She had taught her to deny herself, and to study to do good in all the relations of life. It is true that the mother had a sweet temper to mould; and a natural ground of good from which quickly sprung into existence the seed she scattered with a liberal hand. Still Anna had her own trials—her own struggles against her natural evils, that would lift their deformed heads often and suddenly, causing her exquisite pain of mind. But such temptations, and the consequent disturbed state, were good for her. They made her humbly conscious, that in herself she was weakness and evil, and that only by resisting evil daily and hourly could she rise into true moral strength and beauty. And it was because she thus, in conscious weakness, strove against all that was not pure, and good, and innocent in herself, that she grew in grace day by day.

After fully deciding in her own mind that it was her duty to remain at home with her mother, who was not in a state to see after any of the children, should they awake and cry, as was often the case, and need attention, she went into her chamber and said,—

"I believe, mother, I will remain at home this evening. I shall not feel happy if I go out, and my unhappiness will arise from a consciousness of not having done right. Do not urge me, for I believe to go would be wrong."

"If you feel so, Anna, I will not say one word. Though I cannot but be grieved to think that you are deprived of the pleasure you would have had at Mrs. Leslie's."

"Not more than I shall gain at home, mother. Young as I am, I have many times proved the truth of what I have often heard you say—that the highest pleasure we ever have, is that inward peace which we all feel when we have denied ourselves some promised gratification for the sake of doing good to others."

The mother's eyes filled with tears as she turned them upon her daughter. She looked, but did not speak the pleasure she felt.

THE MAIDEN.

A domestic came in at the moment, and said that a gentleman had called for Anna.

"Mr. Gardiner, I suppose," Anna said, as she arose and left the room.

It was Mr. Gardiner, whom she found in the parlour.

"Good evening, Miss Lee!" he said, in a slightly disappointed tone, as Anna came in. "Are you not going to Mrs. Leslie's?"

"No; she replied; "I am sorry that you have been at the trouble to call for me. Mother has been quite unwell all day, and I do not think I ought to leave her."

"So you do not intend going?" This was spoken in a still more disappointed voice.

"No, I cannot go to-night. It would be wrong for me to leave my mother, and I try never to do anything that I clearly see to be wrong."

But this noble-minded declaration did not awaken in the breast of Gardiner a responsive admiration. He was disappointed, and he could not conceal the feeling.

After sitting for about ten minutes, the young man went away. The interview was not pleasant to either of them. To stay at home from a party just because her mother was not very well, he considered rather a stretch of filial duty; and she, perceiving the true character of his thoughts, shrunk from him instinctively.

From that time Anna received his attentions with

embarrassment. She did not reason much about it. She only felt repulsed. And that all this was right will be seen in the next chapter.

Shortly after Gardiner left, Mr. Lee came home. Anna was still sitting in the parlour, in a musing attitude.

"Why, how is this, Anna? I thought you were going to Mrs. Leslie's to-night," he said with kind interest, sitting down by her side.

"And so I was. But, you know, mother has had a sick headache all day."

"Yes. How is she to-night?"

"She's a great deal better."

"Then, why couldn't you go?"

"Because the children are very apt to get fretful and troublesome, and sometimes won't let any one see them to bed but mother or me. So I thought it best to give them their suppers first, and get them quietly put away for the night. After that was done, I began to fear that they might wake up, as is often the case, and require attention; and I knew if mother went to see to them, her headache would return. She needs quiet and rest. These will be everything to her. If I had gone out, and anything had occurred on account of my absence, to bring back her illness, I should have felt very unhappy indeed."

"You have done right, my dear," said Mr. Lee kissing affectionately the fair cheek of his daughter. "I am sorry that you have been deprived of the enjoyment you would have had at Mrs. Leslie's; but it is all for the best. Even in the least things of our life, as I have often before told you, there is a Providence."

"I believe it, father. Already it has occurred to me, that is for some good that I have been prevented from going this evening."

"It doubtless is, my child," returned Mr. Lee. "Good always springs from a denial of ourselves in order to benefit others. Ever think thus—ever act thus—and ministering angels will draw near to you, and guard you from evil."

Mr. Lee's voice trembled slightly as he said this.

"But I must go up and see your mother," he added; and turning from Anna, he ascended to Mrs. Lee's chamber.

CHAPTER II.

GARDINER'S TRUE CHARACTER EXHIBITED.

HERBERT GARDINER was the son of a retired merchant, who had gained in trade a very large property. Herbert, his only child, had received all the advantages of education that wealth can give; although it cannot be said that he had improved those advantages in any remarkable degree. He was bright enough, as regards intellect; but a high motive for study was wanting.

His father's wealth and social standing left him but little to strive for.

Old Mr. Gardiner had started in life without friends or capital, and had, by honest industry and steady perseverance, worked his way up, until he stood side by side with the most successful. He had a just estimate of the virtues by which he had risen in society, and often strove to impress his son with a deep regard for them. But his precepts did not take very deep root in the ground of the young man's mind.

As soon as he came home from college, he was placed in a mercantile house. He did not, however, take much interest in the business, although, more to meet the requirements of his father than anything else, he attended to his duty sedulously enough to prevent his employers from becoming so much dissatisfied with nim as to dismiss him. After he became of age, his father proposed that he should go into business with some one who had less capital, but a more thorough knowledge of trade than he possessed. Such a person was not hard to find. A young man, whose only capital was business capacity, honesty, and energy of character, soon presented himself. With him a co-partnership was formed, and a capital of five thousand pounds was placed in the hands of the new firm.

Satisfied with the part he had done—or, the part that had been done for him, namely, furnishing capital

—Gardiner did not see that there were very strong claims on him for personal application. He attended at the office daily, and took a certain part in the general operations that were going on, but did not burden his mind with any details, nor trouble himself with any care as to the ultimate result of their operations. He had confidence in his partner, who, glad to get capital to work with, prosecuted the business with vigour and success, for mutual benefit. As for Gardiner, he took his pleasure in his own way. His most favourite companions were not of the safest kind, nor was his own moral character likely to be elevated by associating with them.

He was about twenty-three years of age when he first met Anna Lee, and became charmed with her beauty. His marked attentions, and the evident pleasure he felt in her society, did not escape the notice of Anna, nor fail to make an impression upon her. And more than this, she was not insensible to the fact, that he moved in a higher circle than any to which her position in society would admit her. He was the son of a retired merchant of great wealth; she the daughter of a man in moderate circumstances, who had to struggle hard to support and educate a large family. It was not long before the thought of Herbert would quicken her pulse, and the sight of him make the blood warmer on her cheek.

His true character, however, was little known to her,

and could she have seen him amid the favourite sharers of his coarse pleasures, and the dissipation in which many of his evenings were spent, she would have dismissed him at once and for ever from her mind. It suited his present purpose, however, to assume a virtuous character.

CHAPTER III.

THE BEAUTY AND POWER OF GOODNESS.

ANNA remained sitting in a slightly pensive mood, in the parlour below, after her father left her. The manner of Gardiner had disturbed her feelings. It opened up to her eyes a new view of his character. It presented him to her from a new point of vision. She had denied herself a desired pleasure for the sake of a sick parent, and he had not approved the act—nay, had clearly disapproved it.

"Have I done right or wrong?" she asked herself.

Then reviewing her conduct, and weighing all the reasons that had decided her course of action, she murmured, "Right," and rose to her feet. The tea-bell rang at the moment, and she ascended to the dining-room, to meet her father and mother with a cheerful, happy face.

"I'll pour out the tea," she said, as her mother came in leaning upon her father's arm. "Take you my place."

"No, dear. I can wait on the table well enough," returned Mrs. Lee.

"But I can do it better. So sit down in my place."

"Yes, dear, you had better," said Mr. Lee. "Even the slight exertion of pouring out the tea may disturb your nervous system too much, and bring back that dreadful pain in your head. Let Anna wait on the table this evening."

Mrs. Lee objected no further, and Anna did the honours of the table.

John was very quiet, and had a thoughtful look. The fact was, remembering that Anna had urged him to eat his supper and go to bed when the other children did, because she wished to go out, and seeing that, although called for, she had yet remained at home, he felt that he had been unkind to one who was always kind to him, and who, on account of his perverseness and ill-nature, had been deprived of an expected enjoyment. Had Anna permitted herself to get angry with John, and been led to speak to him from such irritation, he would have remained indifferent. But the gentle forbearance and self-denial of his elder sister touched the boy, and awakened his better feelings. After tea he called her aside, and told her he wanted to go to bed, and that he was sorry he had not done as she wished him to do before. She forgave him with a kiss, when the boy threw his arms round her neck and burst into tears.

"You are so good, and I am so bad," he sobbed. "O sister, I wish I could be so good as you are."

With kind words Anna soothed her brother's mind, and urged him, in future, to try and love all around him, and to be obedient to the wishes of those who sought to do him good. He promised never to disregard what she should say to him, and to strive to conquer his bad temper.

She kissed the penitent boy again, and he went up to his chamber, with subdued feelings, but strong resolutions, to do right in future.

"What a dear good girl our Anna is," said Mr. Lee, after Anna, on leaving the tea-table, had been drawn out of the room by John.

"She is a blessing to our house," returned Mrs. Lee, earnestly. "What should I do without her? For my sake, she has denied herself the pleasure of going to Mrs. Leslie's to-night, although she had made every preparation, and had promised herself, I know, much enjoyment. I urged her not to think of me; but she was firm, and presented her reasons in such a way, that I could not strongly oppose her."

"She has acted from a sense of right, and I am glad that she has done so."

"I cannot but say the same, although my feelings have pled strongly for her; and I have felt sad to think that my indisposition was the cause of her disappointment."

"To me," returned the husband and father, "this

little incident, trifling as it may seem, has given a deeper satisfaction than anything that has occurred for a long time. I see in it the true safe-guard for our child, in this the most critical period of her life. If a self-denying preference of duty to pleasure supply the mainspring of her actions through life, she will be safer against the world's alluring snares, than by any care which we can bestow. In this I trust we may trace the evidences of that true principle of vital Christianity, which can alone supply a never-failing defence against the temptations that beset us here."

When Anna re-entered the room, and their eyes rested upon her face, it was with warmer affections, mingled with something of pride.

CHAPTER IV.

TRUE MAIDEN DELICACY AND ITS OPPOSITE CONTRASTED.

"WHAT in the world kept you away from Mrs. Leslie's?" said a young friend and companion, about her own age, who called in to see Anna Lee on the next day. Her name was Florence Armitage. "We had a most delightful time. Everybody was asking for you, and everybody was disappointed at your absence. I was afraid you were sick, and have called in to see. What *did* keep you away?"

"Mother was not well, and I did not think it right to go out and leave her."

"Was she very ill?"

"She had one of her violent attacks of headache, and was in bed nearly all day."

"I'm sorry. But did that keep you at home?"

"Yes. The children were to look after, and I knew if I were out of the way, and mother not able to attend to them, that there would be trouble. Something, I was afraid, might occur to disturb her mind, and bring back the headache; and then she would have been sick all night. I would rather have missed a dozen parties than that should have happened."

Florence did not seem altogether satisfied that the mere fact of her mother's not being well was a sufficient reason why Anna should forego the pleasures of company. But she did not say this. She only remained silent for a moment or two, and then began to speak of the delightful time they had had.

"I do not know when I have spent a more pleasant evening," she said. "We missed you very much. And that is not all. Your absence deprived us of the company of another, whose presence all would have welcomed. Or, at least, it was the opinion of some of us that such was the case. Mr. Gardiner was not there." And as Florence said this she looked at Anna with an arch smile.

The latter could not prevent a soft blush from stealing over her face, and her eyes were again cast upon the floor. Lifting them, however, after a thoughtful pause, she said to her friend in a serious voice,—

"Are you sure Mr. Gardiner was not there?"

"He came, it is true; but only stayed a little while. It was almost as good as if he had not been there at all."

"But you ought not to say my absence kept him away."

"No. Only that your absence caused him to go away;" replied her friend, smiling.

"You have no right to draw such an inference, Florence. I would much rather it should not be done. I am yet too young to have my name associated with that of any young man."

"How old are you, pray? Perhaps I have mistaken your age. Are you fifteen yet?" continued Florence, in the same sportive mood. "I know you like young Gardiner," she continued. "You can't help it. And all I blame you for is, that you did not go to Mrs. Leslie's with him."

"And neglect a sick mother?"

"It was not any serious matter, that you know well. Only a sick headache. You could have gone well enough."

"Not with a clear conscience, Florence, and without that, I could not have been happy anywhere. External circumstances are nothing in the scale of happiness, if all be not right within. I can say from my heart, that

I enjoyed myself far more at home than I could possibly have done at Mrs. Leslie's, no matter who was or was not there."

"You do not deny, then, that you like young Gardiner?"

"I said nothing in regard to him. Why should I deny or affirm on the subject? I do not know anything about him. I have only seen him a few times in company; and I would be a weak one, indeed, either to think or wish myself beloved by a man who is almost a total stranger."

"He is no stranger. Does not every one in the city know his family and standing?"

"But what do you or I know about him?—of his feelings, character, or principles?"

"You are a strange girl to talk, Anna."

"I think not. Is it not of importance to know something of the governing principles of the man whose attentions are received?—who is admitted, in a character so marked and peculiar, to your intimacy?"

"Certainly. But, then, it is easy enough for any one to see, at a glance, what a young man is. I can do so. There is young Hartley, for example, whom we both know. It is no hard matter to see what he is."

"How do you estimate him?"

"As a very narrow-minded person. I do not like him at all."

"Why?"

"I have just said; because he is narrow-minded."

"That is, you think so. Now, I differ in opinion, judging from the few opportunities I have had of observing him. I should call him a young man of strong good sense, and one who could never stoop to a mean action."

"You do not know him as well as I do."

"Perhaps not. As before intimated, I do not think much about the characters of young men."

"It seems you have thought about Hartley's character."

"My opinion of him is only one of those first impressions which are usually received by us all. I have met him some three or four times; and in every conversation I have had with him, I have been pleased to remark a strong regard for truth and honour, and a generous feeling towards every one, except those who deliberately do wrong."

CHAPTER V.

THE MAIDEN'S FIRST STRONG TRIAL.

SINCE last meeting with Gardiner, Anna had examined her own heart closely; she had thought much about him, and endeavoured to analyze his character as accurately as possible. The result was a distinct conviction, that, although she could not but feel an interest in him, he was not one whose moral feelings harmonized with her own. The glimpse she had obtained of his character, when she told him she must remain at home on account of her mother's illness, was enough to cause her to shrink from him.

In meeting him again, she could not but manifest the reserve and coldness she felt. This disturbed him; and his disturbed feelings reacted on hers, and thus drove them further asunder. When they parted that night both felt unhappy.

From this time, Gardiner, who was piqued at Anna's coldness, was resolved to win her. The very indifference she manifested only confirmed his purpose.

He called frequently on Mr. Lee, and managed often to throw himself into his company in a business way. In every interview, Gardiner was exceedingly polite and deferential; the effect of which on the father's mind could hardly fail to be favourable.

As for Anna, the oftener she met with the young man the stronger became her dislike to him. She could not tell why; but her heart shrunk from him more and more daily.

One evening she was sitting at her piano, and playing over some favourite piece of music, when a domestic came in, and said that her mother, who was alone in her room, wished to see her.

Anna went up, as desired.

"Sit down, dear, I have something I wish to say to you."

The manner in which Mrs. Lee spoke caused the heart of Anna to sink heavily. There was something strange and ominous in it. She dropped into a chair by her mother's side, and looked earnestly in her face. Something half whispered to her the nature of what she was to hear.

"Your father, Anna, who went out a little while ago, wishes me to say to you," began the mother, in a voice that was neither clear nor composed, "that Mr Herbert Gardiner has asked of him the privilege of claiming, with your consent, your hand in marriage."

The maiden rose quickly to her feet, and stood with a quivering lip before her mother.

"You have no doubt expected as much, Anna," added Mrs. Lee, after a pause. "Mr. Gardiner has visited you frequently of late."

Anna tried hard to speak, but it was nearly a minute before she could articulate. At length she said, in a tremulous voice, the tears starting from her eyes as she spoke,—

"Mother—dear mother! Do not speak to me of that. I love you too well to wish to part from you."

And she sunk by her mother's side, and hid her face in her lap. Mrs. Lee was deeply moved. She placed one hand tenderly upon Anna's head, and, with the other, clasped the hand of her child that had fallen upon her bosom. For some time all was still. Then Mrs. Lee endeavoured to raise Anna from her recumbent position; with some difficulty she succeeded in doing so, and placing her in a chair by her side. But the face of the maiden remained concealed in her hands.

"Anna, dear," again began the mother, "I respond with deep tenderness to the love you express. It will be a sad day for me when I am called upon to give you up. But I cannot hide from myself the fact that I shall have to meet and go through the trial, sooner or later. I will not shrink from it, even if it should be to-morrow, if your best interests are concerned."

There was a pause, but no reply. Mrs. Lee resumed,—

"Let your mother speak to you freely. She loves you best. Heretofore she has always communicated with you unreservedly. Let her do so now. Be calm. Be a woman. Meet this subject, the most important in your life, with unruffled feelings. As I before said, Mr. Gardiner has declared to your father that he wishes to address you with views of marriage. He, in fact, through your father, offers you his hand. Do you accept it?"

There was a breathless silence.

"Speak, my child! What is your decision?"

"If left to my decision, mother, it is soon made," was the murmured reply.

"It rests with you, of course."

A quick shudder passed through the maiden's frame,

which was distinctly felt by Mrs. Lee. Then she said, in a firm voice,—

"I decline his offer!"

"Anna!" and Mrs. Lee half started to her feet in surprise.

"Did you not say that I was to decide?"

"True. But how can you decide against *him*, of all others?"

"Because, of all others, I least regard him. The oftener I see him, the more strongly I am repulsed by him."

"Why?"

"I cannot tell."

A long silence followed, during which the mother's mind gradually became clear, and its perceptions distinct. Both herself and husband had been greatly pleased at the offer of Gardiner, and neither of them had entertained the most remote idea that Anna would have declined it. In doing so as promptly as she did, Mrs. Lee was thrown back upon herself, disappointed and confounded. But her good sense, just perceptions, and genuine affection for her child, restored, gradually, her mind's true tone and balance.

"It is for you, and you alone, Anna," she at length said, in a serious, yet affectionate voice, "to decide this matter, and your decision must settle the question. But in making it, have you well considered?"

"Mother, I have. Though too young to be called

upon to decide a matter of so much importance, I have yet been compelled to do it; and it has not been without many a hard struggle, and many an earnest prayer for guiding light to Him whose wisdom is a lamp to **our feet.** I cannot **say I** have not been tempted strongly to make the decision **in his** favour."

"You knew, then, of his intended proposition?"

"No. But I heard from a mutual friend that he was visiting me with serious intentions of marriage, if I would consent, which seemed to be thought a matter of course. At that time I weighed the matter well, and shortly afterwards decided my course. Nothing has **since** occured to make me waver, but rather to confirm my resolution. The oftener I meet him, the more repulsive does he seem to me. Sometimes I have a feeling of suffocation when in his company. And never do I come into his presence without sending up an almost involuntary prayer for wisdom and humble trust in the providential care of my heavenly Father."

Mrs. Lee drew her arm tightly around her child. She was a woman with a true heart and enlightened perceptions, and was therefore satisfied that Anna was not governed by any childish impulse. Feeling thus, not the honour nor wealth of the world could have tempted Mrs. Lee to sacrifice her child.

In about an hour Mr. Lee was heard coming in at the street door; and Anna, first kissing her mother tenderly, glided up to her own chamber. Closing the door after her, she sunk down by her bedside upon her knees, and remained in that attitude for nearly half an hour. When she arose, her face was very pale, but elevated in expression, and beautiful to look upon. Seating herself by the window, she lifted her eyes to the pure sky, jewelled with its myriad stars, and bathed in the soft moonlight. There was about her feelings a holy tranquillity—a deep consciousness of having acted right in a matter involving most vital consequences. The scene accorded with her feelings. Her state of mind was such that nature could speak to her heart, with its low but earnest voice, in language free from perverted human passion. She listened to this voice. Her heart felt its breathings, and answered to them as the murmuring Æolean answers to the gentle breeze that seeks caressingly its yielding strings.

"This is my first strong trial;" thus she thought after a time—"the first temptation my woman's heart has had to endure. How easily might I have fallen into this snare, but for the early instructions, and the example set me by a true-minded mother. She gave me right principles by which to estimate all things around me, and guided my opening affections to things pure and elevated. Had I not been blessed with such a mother—so wise, so thoughtful, so judicious—my weak heart might have been dazzled by a brilliant offer, and I led to accept it, to the destruction of all my best hopes here, and perhaps hereafter."

Anna slightly shuddered as this idea came vividly before her mind.

Some readers may think that the little knowledge Anna had of the character of Gardiner was not enough to cause her to feel, in rejecting his suit, so strongly as here represented. Let such an one know, that a maiden with moral feelings as pure and unselfish as were those of Anna Lee, needs but to have a corner of the veil lifted in order to enable her to determine the quality of a lover's mind. As the quality of the whole ocean may be determined by that of a single drop, so may she, by a single clearly-seen phase of his moral character, determine its whole nature. And Anna Lee did so. Not fully, at first, but undoubtingly; when, added to her rational convictions, came an instinctive feeling of repulsion towards him, as one who was impure and deeply selfish.

CHAPTER VI.

TRIED AND PROVED.

ANNA shrunk from meeting her parent on the next morning. What her father's views of the course she had taken would be she could not tell. She believed that he would not for a moment hesitate to approve of her declaration; and yet doubt would cross her mind, and disturb her young heart to its very centre.

When the breakfast bell rung, she descended from her chamber. Her first glance was at her mother's face. The expression of that told her instantly that all was not right. She did not look at her father for some time after. At length her eyes sought his countenance; it was thoughtful and somewhat stern. What could it mean? Did he wish her to marry a man against whom her whole heart revolted? It could not be. Yet why this change?

So deeply did the unhappiness evidently felt by her mother, and the stern look of her father, affect Anna, that she found it impossible to swallow her food, and soon retired from the table.

Before Mr. Lee left the house, he took his wife aside, and said, in a serious voice,—

"Anna, you must not let this matter go to rest at once. An offer of marriage, such as this, can never be had again for our daughter. Think—Herbert Gardiner is the only son of one of our wealthiest and most esteemed citizens! The character of the family is untainted, and that of the young man, as far as my knowledge goes, unexceptionable. What folly, then, for our child to refuse such an offer!"

"External advantages!" replied Mrs. Lee, "what are these, my dear husband, when set against internal discordance? Nothing! nothing! Dust in the balance! As the mother of Anna, I would rather see her laid, in her maiden sweetness, in the grave, than become the wife of a man for whom she has so strong a feeling of repulsion as that entertained towards Gardiner,—no matter what external advantages might be offered."

Mr. Lee looked grave. The offer of Gardiner had flattered a certain weakness in his character, and obscured the good sense for which he was distinguished. Mrs. Lee had also felt greatly pleased. But her interview with Anna had made all right, so far as she was concerned.

The conversation which passed between the father and mother on the preceding evening was perhaps the most unpleasant ever held by them. Mr. Lee would not listen to Anna's objection, and Mrs. Lee was equally firm in sustaining her daughter in the position she had taken. The discussion was kept up for a long time, and ceased at last, not in the settlement of the difference, but in the unsatisfied and unhappy silence of both parties. The morning, it has been seen, presented the affair in no better aspect.

Still unreconciled to his daughter's objection to Gardiner, Mr. Lee left home, and went to his office. Nothing more passed between Anna and her mother on the subject during the morning. Both avoided speaking about it. At dinner-time Mr. Lee was grave and silent. His manner affected Anna so painfully that she was obliged to leave the table. As she did so, her father glanced at her, and saw that her eyes were not only full of tears, but that large drops were falling over her cheeks.

Anxiously did Anna wait for his return at evening, in order, once more, to look into his face, in the hope that its coldness would have passed away. But the more Mr. Lee thought about the matter, the more he was dissatisfied. There was, therefore, no light in his countenance for his daughter's eye. There still rested a heavy cloud upon his brow. This continued for three days; at the end of which period he was to give an answer to the application made by Gardiner. The nearer the time approached for meeting the young man, the more unhappy did Mr. Lee appear in the presence of his family. On the morning of the day on which a reply to Gardiner's proposition was to be given, he seemed unusually grave. Poor Anna was wretched. Never in her life had she suffered so acutely. She loved her father with the purest feelings—with the deepest tenderness; there was no sacrifice that she dared make, that would not have been cheerfully made for his sake. But more had been asked than she could in conscience do; for with her the marriage rite was felt to be a religious obligation, and the marriage union one that should be made in the sight of Heaven,—thus she had been taught to regard them by her mother, who, since she anticipated such a proposition, had sought, gently and almost unconsciously to her child, to lead her to think of marriage as one of the most sacred acts of a woman's life.

There were times, it is true, when she felt like yielding to her father's wishes, or to what she had the strongest reasons for believing were his wishes—of giving herself up, passively, if her heart were crushed in doing so. But the precepts of her mother had been too deeply stored in her mind. She understood clearly, that, in the sight of Heaven, she dared not make such a sacrifice; that marriage was too holy a thing to be perverted.

Anna knew that on this day an answer would have to be given to Mr. Gardiner—and she therefore understood why her father seemed more than usually oppressed in his feelings. After he had gone out, she went up to her own room, and there spent the whole morning alone. Anxiously did she await his return at dinner-time. As the hour of his coming approached, the unhappy girl became more and more wretched. An undefined fear took hold of her—a dread of some impending evil. When the clock struck three, and she heard, soon after, her father's well-known footstep along the passage, and on the stairs, her heart stood almost still. Mr. Lee went direct to his wife's chamber. Ten minutes more of anxious suspense passed, when Anna heard the ringing of her mother's bell. A domestic went up to her room; then the steps of the same domestic were heard ascending to her chamber. The door opened.

"Your mother wishes to see you."

The maiden started, and turned as pale as death;

but she obeyed the summons, though with a sinking heart. At her mother's door she paused for nearly a minute, and strove, by a powerful effort, to subdue her agitated feelings; but she strove in vain. When she entered, she was hardly conscious of anything beyond a fear of something undefined. But her eyes sought instantly her father's face. A great change had taken place. Instead of the stern, cold, offended look that his countenance had worn for three days, it was subdued, and tender, and full of affection. He reached his hand towards her, and she sprang into his arms, and sunk weeping upon his bosom.

"Dear father! you love me still!" she at length murmured, lifting her head, and looking him in the face.

"Love you, my child! I have always loved you; but now more deeply than ever."

"Then I am happy—happy!" she said, again letting her head fall upon his breast. "I want no other love but the love that makes this home so sweet. It is the first love—the best love—and the most unselfish of all."

Mr. Lee drew his arm tightly around his child, as a response to the sentiment she had just uttered.

"Yes, my daughter," he said, "the loves that make our childhood's home happy are the most unselfish. May they be long continued to us!"

"Amen," was the solemn response, breathed half

involuntarily, yet sweetly, by the maiden, as she clasped tightly her father's hand.

Mrs. Lee's eyes were full of tears; but her whole face **was** elevated and **glad.** She looked calmly on the scene passing before her, silently lifting her heart in thankfulness for so good a child.

"Will you pardon the late strangeness of my manner towards you, Anna?" Mr. Lee said, **after** a little while, raising his daughter up, and looking into her face.

"Do not speak of it, father," she returned, quickly. "If you love me—if you do not blame me—if you will let me still call this **my** home, and you my best beloved, I ask no more. My cup will be full; full to the brim."

"Blame you, Anna? No! If there has been any blame, I must bear it. You have been right. Love you? **We** cannot **tell** you how much we **love you.** And may the day be far distant when you shall go to another home!"

"You have made me happier, dear father, than I have ever been," Anna said, struggling to hide the emotion that was swelling in her bosom. "Do not again feel offended with me. You have taught me to act from a sense of right in all I do,—you have wisely sought to elevate my understanding, and have given me principles by which to determine all my actions. These principles I will ever strive to make rules of conduct. By them I will seek to determine between right

FATHER AND DAUGHTER RECONCILED.

Page 43.

and wrong; and, choosing the right, I will endeavour to abide by it, in all firmness and conscientiousness."

"Do so, my child, even if your father, strange as such a thing may be, should rise up in opposition. Obey him just so far as he wishes you to obey the truth he has taught you, but no further. You are now a woman, and by your own acts you must be justified or condemned. Take no step in life without a clear perception that it is right. Seek aid and light from all who are wiser than yourself, but let their *wisdom* guide you, if guided by others at all. If you cannot see with them, do not act from them. Avoid this, as you would a great evil."

After a slight pause, Mr. Lee added,—

"I saw Mr. Gardiner to-day, and declined for you his offer. Deeply thankful am I that you had the resolution to refuse him. You acted with true wisdom, and a noble firmness that I shall ever admire. Of all that occurred, your mother will inform you at another time."

CHAPTER VII.

A DISAPPOINTMENT.

WHEN Mr. Lee went to his office on the morning of the day named as that on which he was to give an answer to Herbert Gardiner, he felt in a very uncomfortable state of mind. The cause for this was twofold.

First, he could not help feeling a strong desire for the proposed union; and second, he felt that the interview with the young man would be an embarrassing one. But it could not be avoided.

He was sitting in his own private room, about eleven o'clock, when Gardiner came in, smiling pleasantly, and bowing with perfect ease and self-possession. But in a few minutes his manner changed. The disturbed state of Mr. Lee's mind was communicated to his own.

"You know the nature of my business, Mr. Lee," he said, after talking indifferently for a short time. "What is the answer I am to receive at your hands?"

"I regret exceedingly," returned Mr. Lee, "to be compelled to decline your very flattering offer; but my daughter is firm in her opposition to our wishes in the matter. We have—"

"Your daughter objects?" the young man said, with an instantly flushed face, rising quickly to his feet. "Humph!"

There was an air of contempt and conscious superiority in the manner of Gardiner that seriously offended Mr. Lee.

"Yes, sir," he said, his own manner also changing, "she objects, and she, doubtless, has good reasons for it; for she never acts from prejudice or caprice."

"Ha! ha! Don't she, indeed?" The young man had lost control of himself, and spoke very contemptuously. He was quick-tempered, proud, and could ill bear opposition. The unexpected rejection of his suit from one whose social position he considered below his own, had chafed him severely. For nearly a minute he returned Mr. Lee's steady gaze; and then turned on his heel and strode from the room.

The father of Anna drew a long breath, as soon as he found himself alone—sat with eyes upon the floor for some time, and then got up, and walked to and fro, in a deeply abstracted mood. While doing so, one of the Directors of the Company, of which he was the President, an intimate friend, came in. He noticed that Lee was disturbed, and inquired the reason; when he related the interview which had just transpired.

"The vain fop!" ejaculated the friend. "And he really had the assurance to offer himself to your sweet Anna?"

"He offered himself," replied Mr. Lee; "but why should that be called assurance?"

"Humph! You certainly do not know him."

"I never heard a breath against him in my life."

"I have, then; and words too. Why, this Herbert Gardiner is totally unfit to be the husband of a pure-minded creature like Anna, or indeed to be permitted to enter the society where she is."

"You speak strongly."

"Not more so than I should speak. It is strange that you have never heard his character. I thought that it was notorious."

"He **is** in business with a very excellent young man."

"Oh, yes! his capital does that. But a business connection and a marriage are two very different things. I might be willing to enter into business relations with a man that I should not like to see the husband of my daughter."

"Very true. But tell me something specific about Gardiner."

"Let it suffice then to say that his **associates are** often of the vilest character, and his habits exceedingly irregular. Depend upon it, he would have cursed your child in marrying her. From all I have seen **and heard** of that young man, I would sooner see Anna in her grave than his wife!"

"I rejoice, however, there is no danger of such a sacrifice. But **why** should he have sought my daughter's hand?"

"It is a tribute to her loveliness. Even one like him could bow before it. **But** the love of mere external grace and beauty by a man without principle is only of brief duration. These do not minister long to his selfishness—and then the flower that charmed for a brief season is thrown aside with indifference, or trampled upon with scorn."

When Mr. Lee returned home, his feelings were widely different from those with which he had left his family in the morning. The reader has seen the change.

CHAPTER VIII.

A WISE SELECTION OF FRIENDS.

About a week after the interview described in the last chapter, a note was left for Anna Lee, containing an invitation for her to spend an evening at the house of Mrs. Leslie. "A few friends are to be present," was added in the note.

"What have you there?" asked Mrs. Lee, coming into Anna's room about ten minutes after, and finding her daughter sitting in a thoughtful mood, with Mrs. Leslie's invitation in her hand.

Anna gave her mother the note. After reading it, she handed it back, and said with a smile,—

"Mrs. Leslie is very kind, always to remember you when she has company."

"Yes."

This response was cold, and made in an equivocal tone. Anna said nothing more, and Mrs. Lee did not refer more particularly to the subject. On the day before the one to which the invitation had referred, Anna said to her mother,—

"After thinking a good deal about it, I have made up my mind not to go to Mrs. Leslie's to-morrow, nor ever again."

"Have you a good reason?"

"Perhaps not one that I could make fully plain to

everybody. But I think you can understand me. I do not *feel* right, when I think of going there."

"There must be *some* reasons for such a feeling."

"And there are. But even these reasons are so linked with feelings, that my mind cannot separate and give them distinctness."

"Freely state to me all your reasons and feelings," said the mother. "Perhaps, together, we can arrive at a distinct, rational conclusion."

"I have liked Mrs. Leslie, because she always seemed pleased to have me visit her, and showed me very kind attentions," Anna remarked. "But, at the same time, there has been something about her that I could not understand, and from which I have felt an involuntary shrinking. She is the intimate friend of Mr. Gardiner; and, I think, must be thoroughly acquainted with his character and habits. She may be a woman of sound principles; but my mind has many doubts. Anyhow, I do not wish to meet Mr. Gardiner, as I certainly shall, if I go to her house." She then described to her mother the general impression left on her mind by her former visits to Mrs. Leslie, and the reasons she had for thinking she might have a purpose in this invitation.

"I now understand you fully," Mrs. Lee said. "You are right in not wishing to go to her house again. I would not have you do so on any account. Such a woman is a young maiden's most dangerous friend.

She should be shunned as carefully as you would shun an open enemy."

"I am glad you feel as I do about going to her house," returned Anna, seeming much relieved. "Between her and me there is nothing really congenial. I take no pleasure in talking all the time about young men; and she seems to think there is no theme so interesting—nothing so pleasant to a maiden's ear."

There was a gay company at the house of Mrs. Leslie on the next evening. But Anna was not there.

CHAPTER IX.

CATCHING HUSBANDS.

Anna Lee sat sewing one morning, a few days after she had declined going to Mrs. Leslie's, when Florence Armitage, gaily dressed, called in to see her. There were many things about Florence that pleased Anna, although she did not approve of much she did and said. Her mother was a weak woman, and her father was too much absorbed in business to pay attention to his family; so that, between them, her home education had been very much neglected, and very badly managed as far as it went. Anna really pitied her for the defects of her character; and, whenever an opportunity occurred, strove to correct them.

"Come, Anna, put up your work," Florence said

"The day is too fine a one to be spent in-doors. I have called on purpose to take you out."

"I am sorry to disappoint you, Florence," Anna returned, smiling, "but I cannot go out to-day."

"Yes, you can, I know. What in the world is there to keep you at home?"

"A great deal. We have a large family; and that makes plenty of work. It is as much as mother and I can do to keep the children's clothes in order, after we get one half of them made by a sempstress."

"One half! You don't pretend to make half of their clothes?"

"Yes. Why not, if we can?"

"Just for the reason that you ought not to make a slave of yourself."

"And I do not. I must be engaged, usefully, all the while, and nothing more useful offers. I should be very sorry, indeed, to sit down and fold my hands in idleness, and put father to the expense of a sempstress in the house for the whole year round. It would injure me, and be a burden to him. I am sure I should not be as happy as I now am, in the consciousness that I am doing only what I ought to do."

"You are a strange kind of a girl, Anna; and yet, I sometimes wish that I were just like you. But I am not, and cannot be, so there is no use in wishing."

Florence Armitage's purpose in calling was to invite Anna to join her in a promenade in one of the gayest thoroughfares, which formed a fashionable resort of those who deemed it an important purpose of life to frequent such scenes of gaiety, to see and be seen. She urged her friend, but in vain, her answer was decided,—

"No, Florence; for one thing I cannot spare the time—and for another, I could not walk out, unless I had a higher end in view than the one you are proposing to yourself. But suppose you lay off your things, and spend the morning with me."

"No, thank you; I have come out for a walk on Chestnut Street, and I must have it. So, good morning, dear, if I am not to have your good company."

Florence rose, as she said this, and moved towards the door. The friends chatted a few minutes longer, standing, and then the visitor departed.

On the evening of that day, Anna Lee sat reading to her father and mother, when one of the domestics came in, and said that a young gentleman was in the parlour, who wished to see her.

"Who is it?" asked Anna.

"He did not tell me his name," replied the domestic.

The maiden cast her eyes to the floor, and thought for a moment; then looking up, she said,—

"Ask him to send up his name, Margaret."

"Had you not better go down, Anna? Perhaps it may be some friend, who will think you rude," Mr. Lee remarked.

Anna thought again, and then replied,—

"I would rather Margaret would get his name."

"Go then, Margaret," said Mr. Lee, who was beginning to feel a deeper respect for his daughter's perceptions of what was right in matters that concerned herself.

"Who can it be, I wonder?" the mother asked, half musingly.

Anna did not reply, but sat with her eyes upon the page of the book she had been reading. In a few moments the domestic returned, and handed her a card. Her cheek flushed the moment she saw the name upon it. With something of indignation in her voice, she said,—.

"Say to him, Margaret, that I cannot see him."

"Who is it?" asked the father and mother at the same moment. Anna handed her father the card.

"William Archer!" he ejaculated, in surprise. "What brings him here?"

"He has asked for me," replied Anna; "but I cannot see him."

"Could you not, then, better let Margaret say that you will thank him to excuse you this evening?" returned Mrs. Lee. "That would be a milder way of refusing to see the young man."

"I would rather she should say to him, from me, that I cannot see him. That is just the truth, and I wish him to know it. I would not sit alone and talk with that young man for anything that could be given me." And the pure-hearted girl shuddered with an instinctive feeling of horror, for his character was too well known.

Nothing more was said, and the domestic conveyed to Archer Anna's precise words. The young man, half prepared for some such answer, since his name had gone up, retired without a remark, or the evidence of a single emotion. But he was deeply chagrined, and felt angry and bitter towards Anna. A muttered threat of revenge passed his lips as he gained the pavement, and strode off at a rapid pace. But the sweet maiden was safe from all harm he might purpose against her in his evil heart. She was surrounded and defended by her own innocence.

And were every maiden so surrounded and defended, she would be as safe, though she were encompassed by a host of those who sought her ruin.

CHAPTER X.

A NEW LOVER.

The reader will remember that mention has once or twice been made of a young man named Hartley.

A few years previous to the opening of our story, James Hartley came to P—— as a poor boy, and obtained, through the recommendation of a friend who knew his family, a situation in a wholesale mercantile house. His honesty, industry, and intelligence, soon made him valuable to his employers, who, as he advanced in years, elevated him in their confidence step by step, until, long before he had reached the age of twenty-one, he occupied the position of their chief and confidential clerk. Never, in the slightest degree, did he betray their confidence, or trespass with undue familiarity upon their frankness, and the open generous manner in which they always treated him. When he became of age, so highly was he esteemed and valued, that he was offered a share in the business, and became one of the firm of R——, S——, & Co., and entitled to a moderate dividend on the profits.

During his minority, the young man had devoted himself so closely to business, and given to it so much of his thoughts, that he had neglected to adorn his mind by tasteful reading, and to furnish himself with stores of general information. On entering into company, at a pretty early age, he became aware of his deficiencies in this respect, and to make up for them as rapidly as possible, he spent most of his evenings in reading and study. Naturally modest, and disposed to think more of his deficiencies than of his attainments, he was retiring in company, and therefore attracted but little attention. He was not much of a favourite with young ladies, because he did not pay them very marked or flattering attentions. This was not the result of intention, but arose from want of confidence in himself, which would have pushed him forward, and made him an agreeable companion to all. As he gradually became better and better acquainted with the different ladies in whose society he was thrown, some liked him, and, indeed, highly esteemed him, while others thought him a dull companion. He had never learned to dance, and this tended to keep him back, and to prevent his circle of acquaintance from enlarging; for while most of the young ladies were on the floor, threading the mazes of the graceful cotillion, he was in some corner, in grave conversation with their mothers, or entertaining some neglected maiden, whom no one thought it worth while to take as a partner.

From these causes, as just said, he was not a general favourite with young ladies. Their opinions in regard to him were various. Some thought him dull and stupid; while others, with whom he had conversed more freely, considered him sensible enough, but narrow-minded in his views and feelings; others, again, said that they thought they could like him very well, but that they never could get near him.

Upon the whole, although no one could allege any moral defect against Hartley, there were very few of the younger members of the social circle who cared to be very gracious towards him, or who did not feel under some constraint when by his side.

Anna Lee first met him after he had been going into

company for a year or two. He was then a member of the house in which he had served his time. From the moment he saw her, Hartley liked Anna; but she was so general a favourite, that it was a rare thing, indeed, that he could get by her side; and when he did, she always showed a reserve that, acting upon his feelings, already prepossessed in her favour, closed up his mental perceptions, and caused him to appear to very poor advantage. Of this he was clearly conscious.

Gradually, as he met Anna Lee again and again in company, Hartley saw more and more of the beautiful order and purity of her character. From pleasure experienced in the observation of these, admiration soon arose in his mind; and this, imperceptibly, as one moral beauty after another unfolded itself to his eyes, deepened into a feeling of earnest regard. At this time he was concerned to observe that Herbert Gardiner, whom he well knew, was beginning to be very marked in his attentions towards Anna; and he was still more concerned to see that his attentions were not apparently disagreeable.

Coolly, and with more philosophy than is ordinarily to be found in young men, Hartley held himself aloof, and looked on to see the result.

"What a fool!" he heard a young friend say, as he came up and joined a group of acquaintances who were standing at the entrance of a neighbour's warehouse one day, not long after he had marked the advances of Gardiner.

"Who's a fool?" he asked.

"Why, that pretty daughter of Lee's."

"What Lee?"

"President of —— Insurance Company."

"Pray, what has she been doing?"

"It is said she has declined an offer made her by Herbert Gardiner."

"Why did she decline him?"

"Some girlish whim, I suppose."

"She did not like his character, it is said," remarked one.

"What does she know about that, I wonder?" returned another.

"Prudish folly!" ejaculated one of the party, turning on his heel, and going off.

The little group separated at this, and Hartley went to his own warehouse. The fact he had heard thrilled him with pleasure, and gave to Anna Lee, in his mind, a far more elevated position than she had before held.

About a month afterwards, during which time he had not once met Anna, he heard of her refusal to receive a call from Archer. Various reasons were assigned for this, but he was very sure that he understood the true one.

"Noble girl!" he said to himself. "Oh, that every honest woman would stamp, as you have done, the seal of displeasure upon vice!"

Firm and consistent in his own conduct, and ever acting from principles of right, settled as truths in his own rational mind, James Hartley was an admirer in all of firmness and consistency; but how much more in one whom his heart had already begun to love! His own person was plain, and Anna had declined an offer from one who was generally admitted to be one of the most fascinating and noble-looking young men in the city. He had not, as some others who would seek her favour, those graces of mind which are so beautiful and attractive. He possessed not riches, although he was well connected in business. His family was obscure; in fact, unknown in the city. He was himself modest and retiring, and could not go forward and extort attention, as many had the power of doing.

These thoughts made him sad with feelings of doubt and discouragement.

CHAPTER XI.

AN IMPRESSION MADE.

"HAVE I not done right, father?" Anna said, looking up earnestly into her father's face, as soon as the street door had been heard to close behind Archer.

"Yes, dear, perfectly right," replied Mr. Lee. Anna's eyes fell again upon the page of the book she held in her hand. Neither her father nor mother made any further remark; and she, after sitting silent for some time, resumed her pleasant task of reading aloud to them. But her voice was neither so clear nor calm as it had been. It was slightly tremulous and husky. She read on, for half an hour, and then shut the book, and left the room. Ascending to her own chamber, and closing the door after her, she sunk upon her knees at the bedside, and lifted up her heart in earnest prayer to be guided aright in all the relations of life; and to be endowed with firmness to act truly her part as a woman.

The incident that had just transpired, and the position she had felt it to be her duty to take, had disturbed her feelings. But now she felt calmer, and more clearly conscious that she had acted right.

The fact that Anna had refused to see, even in her own house, the young man who had called upon her, soon became known and talked about.

Many a gay flatterer, who had before flitted around her, kept at a distance. All this favoured our friend Hartley. Anna was more accessible to him in company, for she was not so frequently as before the partner of some gay friend.

The more intimately Anna knew Hartley, the more she thought about him. There was something, to her eye, beautiful in the honest simplicity of his mind, and attractive in the moral strength of his character. At first he had seemed a common man. She had responded to his attentions, whenever she was thrown into his company, because she was kind to all who were worthy of kindness; but as she met him oftener, knew him better, and marked the orderly character of his mind, and the healthy tone of his sentiments, she could not but admire him. And when he ventured to call to see her at her father's house, she received his visit with pleasure, although she had not the most distant suspicion that his call was anything more than a friendly visit.

After he had gone away, Anna sunk down upon the sofa in the parlour alone, and fell into a dreamy musing state of mind. Many images, dim and but half defined, floated before her; and mingled with them was the form of young Hartley. She heard the sound of his voice, and remembered many sentiments he had uttered. And all this was pleasing to her.

The young man trod the pavement, as he walked homeward, with light footsteps, and a lighter heart. Anna had not refused to see him. And more than that, she had sung and played for him—the music sounding sweeter to his ears than anything he had ever heard—and seemed interested in all the conversation that passed between them.

In a week Hartley called again. But this visit was far from being as pleasant as the first. Anna seemed reserved. What could it mean? Had she suspected his feelings? And did she mean to repulse him?

The thought embarrassed him, and made their intercourse, during the hour that he stayed, unsatisfactory to both.

The young man did not venture upon a third visit. He was afraid. The coldness of Anna, it was evident to his mind, arose from a dislike towards him, and he shrunk from the direct issue of an open repulse.

Two months passed, and not once during that time had Hartley ventured to call upon the maiden who was in all his waking and dreaming thoughts. Two or three times he had met her upon the street, and, although she had spoken to him, there was something shy about her—something altogether unusual in her manner. He interpreted it to mean a dislike for him; but he was a young man, and little acquainted with the language of a woman's heart.

CHAPTER XII.

WOOED AND WON.

Soon after, Hartley, who could not erase the image of Anna Lee from his mind, determined, in a moment of half desperation, to call upon her once more.

"If she dislikes me, I will see it, and I want some certainty," he said to himself.

Under this feeling he visited her.

"Mr. Hartley is in the parlour," said a domestic, as

she opened the door of the room where Anna was sitting with her parents.

Mr. Lee looked into the face of his daughter, and saw that the announcement had disturbed the quiet tone of her feelings. But whether the effect were pleasing or otherwise, he could not tell.

"Tell him I will be down in a few minutes," Anna said, rising. She took a light and went to her own room, where she rearranged her hair, put on a collar, and made some trifling alterations in her dress. She lingered a few minutes after this, to give her feelings, which were more than ordinarily ruffled, time to calm down. Then she descended to the parlour.

Hartley had been waiting for her in a state of nervous uncertainty. Upon the character of her reception of his visit hung all his hopes. If she smiled upon him, he would be the happiest man in existence; if she repulsed him by her manner, he would be the most miserable. He was in this state of mind when Anna came in, and advancing towards him, offered her hand with a graceful face, and a manner so frank and warm, that the young man took instant courage. In a little while they were conversing together perfectly at ease, and each interested in and silently approving the sentiments uttered by the other. When they separated, both felt happier than they had been for weeks. Why it was so with Anna, she hardly dared to acknowledge to herself. To Hartley, as far as he was concerned, the matter was plain as daylight. He did not suffer many days to elapse before calling again. To his great delight he was received as kindly as before; and even half-blind as he was from over-modesty and bashfulness, could see that there was something warmer in the face and eyes of the maiden than expressed an ordinary friendly feeling towards an acquaintance. He now visited Anna regularly, and was ever a welcome guest.

On one occasion, after Hartley had paid close attention to her for two or three months, there was a freer exchange of sentiments, and the conversation was upon subjects that brought out from both an expression of the leading principles that ought to govern in the common affairs of life. Hartley was pleased to find that Anna had sound views upon all the questions that came up; and she was no less gratified to perceive in him, as she had often before perceived, a basis of good sense, a clearly discriminating mind, and a love of truth for its own sake. They had been speaking of the beauty of moral excellence, when Anna remarked—and she did so to see how far his principles led him,—

"But to come to the real truth at last, Mr. Hartley, moral excellence is nothing, if it be not the result of Christian principles in the heart."

Hartley looked at the maiden, but did not reply.

"In fact," she resumed, "unless all our actions are regulated by divine love, our morality has but a slender base to stand upon—is, in fact, only an assumed and not a real morality, and when the storms of temptation arise, and the floods beat against it, it will fall."

He still remained a silent but admiring listener, and she went on,—

"A man may render civil obligations to his country, because his interest is involved in doing so; and he may act in all the varied relations of life with external faultlessness, and yet not be in heart a good man or a good citizen. He may obey the laws, because he thereby secures his own good; and he may be hospitable, and kind, and generous from a love of the world's good opinion; but, if he could believe that it would be more to his interest to violate the law, what would hold him in obedience to that law? Or, if he were placed in circumstances where he could not forfeit or gain the world's good opinion, would he be generous and hospitable? But, if he is a good citizen, and a moral man from religious principle—that is, if he be actuated by the pure and lofty principles of a disciple of Christ, seeking in the diligent pursuit of business, no less than in the privacy of his closet, to serve God, then will he be in reality a good citizen and a truly upright man. Is it not so, Mr. Hartley?"

"Doubtless all you have said is true," returned the young man. "But who around us is thus governed by religious principles?"

"Many, I hope."

"Can you name one?"

The maiden's cheek became slightly suffused as she replied, after a moment's hesitation,—

" Yes; one at least."

" Who is it ? "

" My father. And it is to him I am indebted for the light that my own mind has received on so important a subject."

" Do you not know another ? "

" I do. My mother acts from the same high obligations."

" And you do the same ? "

Hartley looked earnestly into his companion's face, as he said this, that not a single varying shade of its expression might be lost.

" I try to do so," was the modestly spoken answer; " but I am conscious, every day, that my efforts are altogether imperfect. That my character is not yet based upon an ever-abiding love of the truth for its own sake."

" I am glad to hear you say so," Hartley returned, with a smile.

" Glad ! " And Anna looked at the young man with surprise.

" Yes, glad. Like you, I am struggling to make the laws of moral and civil life one with the laws of divine order ; but my efforts are imperfect, and my progress very slow. Sometimes I seem not to advance at all. Is not that your own experience ? "

"It is; and I sometimes fear will ever be. Yet we must remember Him who promises that his strength shall be made perfect in our weakness. But why should you be glad at my imperfections?"

Hartley ventured to take her hand. She yielded it passively. Looking steadily into her mild, blue eyes, he said,—

"Because I feared that you were perfect; and if so, I should have been without hope."

The eyes of the maiden fell suddenly. A burning blush covered her whole face, yet she did not withdraw the hand that was held by her companion.

"But like myself, you are conscious of imperfections —conscious of weakness and evil, and, like myself, are struggling to rise above them," continued Hartley, tightening his hold upon the small, soft hand that lay so passively in his. "Shall we not help each other to rise into a higher and better life? Shall we not, together, struggle with temptation, and together find a Sabbath rest when we have conquered? Shall we not strive to find that strength from on high which we have not in ourselves, and seek from our blessed Saviour, and by the right he hath purchased for us by his own blood, that most precious of all gifts, the Holy Spirit?" His voice deepened under the excitement of the moment, and the earnestness of his own feelings; and Anna thought he had never before seemed so worthy of her love. He once more appealed to her to respond to his feelings, but her look showed that no words were needed to assure him of her sympathy and unity with him.

Anna could not reply; but her heart was fluttering with joy. She could only let her hand remain in that of her lover; and she did let it remain, and even returned his tight clasp with a gentle pressure.

When Hartley passed from the door of Mr. Lee's dwelling, he was bewilderingly happy. Anna had consented, with her parents' approbation, to accept his hand in marriage.

CHAPTER XIII.

CONCLUSION.

ANNA'S wedding-day quickly came. To her it brought mingled feelings of pleasure and sadness. The maiden was about to take upon herself a wife's duties, to enter upon an untried sphere of action. To step from the peaceful happy home of her father into the dwelling of a husband. To begin a new life of deeper and more varied emotions.

Towards her mother, whom she was about to leave, she felt an unusual tenderness; for she realized, in her own mind, how lonely that mother would be when she was away; and there were moments when, from this reason, she half regretted having named so early a wedding-day. Then her thoughts would turn to the children over whom her care had been exercised, ever since they were babes in their mother's arms. She loved them truly—how could she leave them? Who could fill to them her place? Such thoughts would at times throw a deeply pensive shade over her feelings. But the intense love she bore the chosen of her heart, would carry away her mind to him, and she would muse with delight over the thought of becoming one with him in marriage.

Thus passed the day, amid preparations for the ceremonies that were to take place in the evening. Anna was musing alone in her room just before nightfall, when her mother came in, and sitting down beside her, took her hand and warmly pressed it within her own. As she did so, the maiden leaned over against her, and let her head rest upon the bosom that had so often before pillowed it, looking up as she did so into her mother's face with eyes swimming in tears of pure filial love.

"You are about to leave us, my dear child," Mrs. Lee said in a voice half inaudible from emotion; and then paused to get a better command of her feelings. Anna closed her eyes to keep the tears from stealing over her face.

"You are about to leave us, Anna," resumed Mrs. Lee, "and I pray that you may be as good a wife as you have been a daughter. I am sure you will. It is hard to part with you, my child, very hard; but it is right that you should go. You are a woman, and must act a woman's part. Act it well, and you will be a blessing to all. I believe the man who has chosen you to be his companion through the journey of life is worthy to claim your hand. I believe he will do all in his power to make you happy. I give you away to your husband with a confidence that few mothers can feel. You must, you will be happy in his love, for he is worthy of you. Oh, believe that you can never be more than worthy of the love of such a man as James Hartley. Cherish the deep affection he has for you with the tenderest care; for a heart like his is a rare jewel—it is priceless in value."

Anna lay close to her mother's breast and quiet as an infant.

More, much more of earnest precept was poured into her ear, to all of which the maiden listened with the most profound attention. Mrs. Lee lifted the veil for her child, and gave her new views of the marriage relation and of her duties in it. When that child descended to the crowded rooms below, some hours afterwards, and plighted her faith before God and man, it was with sober feelings, and a strong internal resolution to act the wife's part truly, difficult as the task might be to perform.

Shall we say more? What more remains to be said? Anna Lee, the pure-hearted Anna Lee, is married to the man of her choice. She has passed safely through the perils of maidenhood, and **is now a wife—and a wife wisely wedded.**

But we must **not lose** sight of **her. As a "Wife" we will** still **follow her, and see how, in her new** relations, she sustains **the harmonious consistency of** character **that made her so lovely as a maiden,** and blessed all who **came within the sphere of her** influence.

[The reader will readily perceive in **what follows that** the story is one of American life; and occasionally narrates conversations and occurrences somewhat at **variance** with the ideas entertained of married life in England.]

The Wife.

CHAPTER I.

AN EFFORT TO BEGIN RIGHT—A WISE DECISION.

JAMES HARTLEY had been married three weeks—three of the happiest weeks he had ever spent; but happier far was his lovely young bride. A form of affection, as every woman is, she could love more deeply, and feel a more intense delight in loving. The more closely she looked into her husband's mind, and the clearer she saw and understood the moral qualities by which it was adorned, the purer and more elevated was her love.

They sat alone, side by side, as the day was drawing to a close, the hand of the wife resting, confidingly, in that of her husband. They were yet in the family of the bride's father, who would not hear of their going away.

" It is plenty of time these three or four months to come for Anna to take upon herself the cares of domestic life," he would say, whenever any allusion was made by either his daughter or her husband to their intention of going to housekeeping.

But both James Hartley and his bride thought differently, as a conversation that passed between them some few days previously will show.

"We have been married now for nearly a month, Anna," remarked Hartley; "and it is full time that we began our preparations for housekeeping."

"A thing, you know, that father will not consent to our doing."

"So it seems. But is it right for us to remain here longer than is necessary to make proper arrangements for getting into our own house?"

"Is there any reason why we should hurry these arrangements?" returned Anna.

"None in the least. We should make them deliberately and wisely."

"And may they not be made as well three months hence as now?"

"You shall answer that question yourself," replied Hartley, smiling. "We are now husband and wife."

A light, like the flitting of a sun-ray over the face of Anna, was the response to this affirmation.

"As such," continued the husband, "we occupy a new, peculiar, and distinct position in society. The sphere of our influence is a different one from what it was. All who approach us are affected differently from what they formerly were. You can understand why this is so?"

"Clearly. All new relations make a corresponding impression on society. The influence of the maiden is one thing, and the influence of the wife another."

"And they act in different spheres."

"Yes. One is on the circumference of the family circle, so to speak, the other in the centre."

"The exact truth. Now, what position does a wife occupy in a family circle of which she is not the centre? An orderly one?"

Anna shook her head.

"If not an orderly one, then not the most useful one —not the true one."

"But I, as a wife, would make both centre and circumference in the family circle now. Or, rather, you and I would."

"Even admitting this, which is not exactly clear, we would both be in truer order than when on the circumference and not in the centre at the same time. You will admit that?"

"I cannot help doing so."

"And if in truer order, in a better way of acting usefully in the world."

"Yes."

"Then, as husband and wife, can we too soon take our true social position? I think not. Life's duties are not so few, that any of them can safely be neglected for a single day. It is very pleasant to live here, without a thought or care about external things. But I am not at all sure that it is good for either of us."

"Nor am I, now that I fully comprehend your views, which I see to be correct in every particular. Father and mother will regret our leaving them, I know. But you are now my husband, and I am ready, when I see truth in your rational mind, to stand up by your side in obedience to the truth, even though all the world should be offended."

"Which, of course, they will not be, at our doing so sensible a thing as going to housekeeping in a month or two after our marriage."

Anna smiled sweetly into her husband's face, as he replied thus playfully to her earnestly-expressed sentiment.

From that time their resolution was taken.

On the occasion referred to in the opening of this chapter, the subject of conversation was their intention of making early preparations for getting into their own house. On the day previous, they had conversed seriously with Anna's father and mother, who, much against their will, could not help yielding a rational consent to the reasons offered by their children for the resolution to take their true place in society.

"There is now a very good house in Walnut Street to rent, which, I think, will just suit us," remarked Hartley, while they sat, hand and hand, as we have seen. "I looked through it to-day, and find that it has every convenience that could be desired. It is just below —— street."

"One of those large, handsome houses?"

"Yes. You remember them?"

"Very well. What is the rent?"

"Eighty guineas."

Anna made no reply, but sat with her eyes cast thoughtfully to the floor. She not only had no wish to go into so large and expensive a house, but felt an instant reluctance at the thought of doing so. She had no certain knowledge in regard to her husband's worldly circumstances, but she did not believe that he was rich. She had been living with her father in a plain and comfortable style, and did not think of anything greatly superior.

Hartley looked earnestly into the face of his young wife, and sought to read its expression.

"How do you like the house I mention?" he at length said.

Here came a trial for Anna, the trial of not agreeing with her husband. Her wish was to yield, in all things, her will to his; but, unless her judgment approved, she could not so yield with a clear conscience. In this matter, her judgment did not approve, and she felt an acute pain at the thought of objecting to his proposal. With an effort, and a look that asked forgiveness for opposition, she said,—

"It is a very handsome house. But—"

And she hesitated, while a warm glow suffused her face.

"But what, dear?" The kindness with which this was spoken re-assured Anna, who felt an inward dread of the effects of opposition. The idea that she should ever be called upon to differ from her husband in anything requiring concert of action, had, until now, never crossed her mind.

"Don't you think the rent too high?" she said, in a suggestive tone.

"Not for the house. It is a very excellent one, and there is not a more desirable situation, I think, in the city."

"But for us to pay, I mean?"

Hartley looked again earnestly into the face of his wife—so earnestly that her eyes dropped beneath his fixed gaze. Another silence followed; to Anna a troubled one.

"I don't know but that you are right," the husband said, with a frank smile. "Eighty guineas is rather a heavy rent for two young people like us to pay."

"But it is not only the rent, dear," returned Anna, brightening up. "A large and elegant house like that must be furnished in a liberal and corresponding style. And then there would have to be a free expenditure of money to maintain such an establishment. For my part I do not desire to come before the world, as a young wife, in so imposing a manner."

Hartley returned to this an approving pressure of the hand he still held.

"Still," resumed Anna, "if your circumstances justify such a style of living, and you desire it, I, as your wife, will not object for an instant."

This remark helped to set Hartley right. The house in which he was partner was doing a heavy business, and there was a prospect of making large profits. If this expectation should be realized, his division would be a handsome one. But if not—that "if" had never before presented itself so distinctly to his mind as at this moment. In thinking about commencing housekeeping, he had felt ambitious to raise Anna to as elevated a condition as possible. To place her alongside of the "best and proudest." All this was more from impulse and feeling than reason. His pride, not his good common sense, was influencing him. At the first blush, although he did not let it be seen, he felt disappointed at the want of cordial approval manifested by Anna, for whose sake, more than his own, he had fixed upon the handsome house in Walnut Street. But the view she took of the subject, so soon as it came directly in front of the eye of his mind, he saw to be the true one.

"That may be a question," he said, in reply to her last remark, speaking thoughtfully. "It is true that everything looks bright just now; but it is also true that clouds often come suddenly over the brightest skies. It was for your sake that I wished to rent that house. I felt a pride in the thought of making you its mistress."

"I shall be much happier as the mistress of a less imposing residence. Let us begin the world without ostentation. As we are about to commence housekeeping from a sense of right, let us not consult appearances, but be governed throughout by the right ends that prompted our first decision. For my part, a house at half, or even less than half the rent of the one in Walnut Street, will meet all my expectations. To manage its internal arrangements will cost me less care and labour, and you less money; and it is needless to be too free with either in the beginning of life."

"Well and wisely said, Anna. I fully agree with you. I yielded to a weakness when I set my heart upon the house I have mentioned. I will look further, and see if I cannot find as many comforts as that presented, in a more compact and less costly form."

"I am sure you will. And I am sure we will be happier than if we had made our *debut* in a much more imposing way."

And thus the matter was settled. The reader cannot but say wisely, when he reflects that James Hartley was without capital himself, and only a junior partner in a mercantile house, which, although it was doing a heavy business, might not at the end of the year, from causes against which ordinary foresight could not guard, divide anything more than very moderate profits. A woman with different views and feelings would never have thought of objecting to become the mistress of an establishment like the one offered by Hartley; but Anna had no weak pride or love of show to gratify. She looked only to what was right; or, at least, ever sought to do so.

CHAPTER II.

A THOUGHTLESS WOMAN OF THE WORLD—FLORENCE ARMITAGE.

"You are going to housekeeping, I hear," said Mrs. Riston, a young friend, about a week after the conversation mentioned in the preceding chapter had taken place. Mrs. Riston had called in to see Anna, whose acquaintance she had recently made.

"Yes," was the smiling reply.

"You'll be sorry for it?"

"Why so?"

"Oh, it will bring you into a world of trouble. My husband has been teasing me to death about going to housekeeping ever since we have been married. But I won't hear of it."

"That is strange. I thought every married woman would like to be in her own house."

"Oh dear! no. I know dozens who would throw

houses and all into the river if they could. It makes a slave of a woman, Mrs. Hartley. She is tied down to a certain routine of duties of the most irksome nature; and this, day in and day out, the year round. And what is worse, instead of her duties growing lighter, they are constantly increasing."

"But all these duties it is right for her to perform, is it not?"

"Not if she can get out of them, or delegate their performance to some one else, as I do. In a boarding-house you pay for having all this trouble taken off your hands. And I think our husbands may just as well pay for it as not. I have no notion of being a slave. I did not marry to become a mere drudge, so to speak, to any one."

"It is a question in my mind, Mrs. Riston, whether it is right to delegate the duties we are competent to perform," was Anna's mild reply.

"All nonsense! Get out of doing everything you can. At the best you will have your hands full."

"No doubt I shall find plenty to do; but my labour will be lightened by the consciousness that it is done in order to make others happy."

"Others happy! Oh, la! Who'll try to make you happy, I wonder?"

"My husband, I hope," said Anna, gravely.

"Humph! You will see. Husbands ain't the most unselfish creatures in the world. I believe they are not proverbial for sacrificing much to the happiness of their wives."

Anna felt shocked at this. But her young friend did not notice the effect her words produced, and continued to run on.

"You had better take my advice, and tell your husband, as I have told mine over and over again, that you are not going to become a domestic slave for him or anybody else."

Anna shook her head.

"Well! Just as you like. If you will go to housekeeping, so be it. It won't hurt me. Have you picked out your house yet?"

"We haven't exactly decided. Mr. Hartley thought at first of taking a very beautiful house in Walnut Street, at a rent of eighty guineas."

"But very soon thought better of it, I have no doubt.

"If I had not objected, he would have taken it."

"You objected? Why so?"

"I thought it would involve more expense and style than two young folks like us ought to indulge in."

"Upon my word! But you are a novice in the world! This is the first instance that has occurred among all my acquaintances of such a thing as a wife objecting to style and expense. Precious few of us get the chance, I can assure you! And you'll soon wish, or I am mistaken, that you had taken your good man at his word."

Anna felt a glow of indignation at this reflection upon her husband. But she forced herself to appear unmoved, merely replying,—

"No; I shall never wish that. I shall never have any want, in his power to supply, that will not be readily met."

"So you may think now. But take my advice, and don't put any prudential and penurious notions into your husband's head. If he wants to carpet your floors with gold, let him do it. He'll never hurt himself by spending money on you or his household. Men rarely, if ever, do, let me tell you. As they grow older, they get to be closer and closer with their money, until at last you can get scarcely anything at all. The best time is at first. The first few years of marriage is the only golden harvest time a woman ever sees."

"You have not been married long enough to speak all this from experience."

"I have seen a good deal more of life than you have, child; and I have had my own experience. As far as it goes, I can witness fully to what I have said. And yet my husband is as good as the rest, and much better than the mass. I love him about as well, I suppose, as most women love their husbands; though I don't pretend to be blind to his faults. But what kind of a house do you prefer, seeing that the elegant one in Walnut Street is rather costly and stylish?"

"There is a house vacant close by. Perhaps you noticed the bill as you came up R—— Street."

"Just round the corner?"

"Yes; the rent is thirty guineas."

"Mrs. Hartley!"

"It is a very good house, and quite genteel, with a great deal more room than we want."

"But, my dear, good madam, it is nothing but an ordinary house, built to rent. There is nothing elegant about it. Don't refuse to take the one in Walnut Street for so common an affair as this, if you can get it. Always aim at the best."

"I have been through it, and find it replete with every convenience for a moderate-sized family. I have no wish to make a display. That would render me no happier. I go to housekeeping, because I think it right to take my true place as the mistress of a family; and for no other reason. Here I could be happy, without a care. But I would be out of my true sphere."

"You are certainly the strangest creature I ever met," replied Mrs. Riston. "But a few years will take all this nonsense out of you."

The displeasure felt by Anna at Mrs. Riston's insinuations against her husband, began to give way, as she saw more clearly the lady's character, and began to understand that, although there was a good deal of earnest in what was said, there was much more of talk for talk's sake. She, therefore, merely replied in a laughing voice to Mrs. Riston's last remark, and sought to change the subject. Before they parted, the friend could not help saying,—

"But, my dear Mrs. Hartley, I cannot get over your refusing that elegant house in Walnut Street. I should like, above all things, to see you in just such a dwelling, elegantly furnished. If I had refused the splendid offer that you did in Herbert Gardiner, I would compass sea and land but I'd show him that I had lost nothing."

This very indelicate and ill-timed remark caused the blood to rush to the brow of Anna, and her eyes to flash with honest indignation. Her volatile friend saw that she had gone a little too far, and attempted to make all right again, by begging "a thousand pardons." Anna's external composure soon returned, but she sought to change entirely the subject of conversation. But, in spite of all she could do, the lady would, ever and anon, have something disparaging to say about husbands, and gently insinuate that Anna herself, before she was many years older, would find that all was not gold that glittered.

The warmth of Anna's feeling gradually, in spite of herself, passed off, as she continued to converse with Mrs. Riston, until she became constrained in her manner. This affected her visitor, who perceived, with a woman's intuition, that her sentiments had not met with the approval they too often did from her lady friends. She tried, before she went away, to soften some things she had said, and laugh at others as having been uttered in jest. After Mrs. Riston's departure, Anna sat in a thoughtful mood for some time. The remarks she had just listened to shocked her feelings more and more the more she reflected on them.

"Can there be any happiness," she mused, "in marriage thus viewed? In the marriage relation thus perverted? I can conceive of none. To me, such a union would be, of all things, a condition most miserable."

While thus musing, another visitor called. It was Florence Armitage. Since her last recorded interview with Anna, she had received a severe lesson. Guided alone by the thoughtless vanity which then appeared to her a sufficient motive of action, she had received the addresses of William Archer, though knowing that his character was not such as a pure-minded woman would desire in her husband. The young man exerted all his powers to render himself agreeable to her, and with such success, that the day was fixed, and everything prepared for their marriage, when an unexpected disclosure proved the baseness of his character, and abruptly broke off all intercourse with him, on the very day appointed for their marriage. Since the severe lesson her heart had received, Florence was a good deal changed. Her thoughtlessness, which had come near involving her in a whole lifetime of misery, and her critical escape, made her feel humble and thankful.

She visited Anna frequently, and profited much more than formerly by her truthful precepts.

On this occasion Anna saw, after a few moments that her friend was slightly agitated.

"You seem disturbed, Florence. What is the matter?" she said.

The colour deepened on the maiden's face.

"Who do you think I met in the street just now?"

"I cannot tell."

"William Archer."

"But you did not recognise him?"

"No."

"In that, I need scarcely say, you were right. Your own heart will tell you that."

"And yet, Anna, I confess to you that I was tempted to do so."

"Florence!" Anna's voice and countenance expressed strongly the surprise she felt.

"Do not condemn me until you hear all; until you know the cause of disturbance. I received a letter from him yesterday."

"Which you immediately returned unanswered?"

"No, I did not feel sure that I ought to do so, until I had seen and conversed with you about it."

"What does he say?"

"Here is his letter; read it."

Anna shrunk from touching the epistle, which Florence held towards her.

"Read it aloud, if you particularly wish me to know its contents," she merely said.

Florence did as requested. The letter contained a most solemn denial of charges brought against the writer by a certain individual, who was, he said, evidently not in her right mind, and whose statements should at least be taken with great caution. He knew that rumour had been busy with his name, and had magnified his faults into crimes; "and how easy it is," he urged, "to blast any man's character by false charges, if he is not permitted to refute them;" with much more of the same tenor. Altogether, the letter was written with tact, force, and an air of great plausibility, and well calculated to create a doubt as to the correctness of the judgment which the general voice had passed upon him. He did not, he said, purpose to renew his suit for the hand of Florence; for that, he was well assured, would be useless. But it was a duty he owed to himself and society to at least make an attempt to vindicate his character, and in the highest quarter.

After Florence had read the letter, she looked inquiringly into the face of Mrs. Hartley. Anna returned her steady look, but made no remark.

"There is, at least, an appearance of truth about this letter," Florence at length said.

Mrs. Hartley compressed her lips and shook her head, but did not speak.

"I am afraid, Anna, that you sometimes suffer your

prejudices to obscure the otherwise clear perceptions of your mind. We are all liable to err, Anna."

"True. But if a woman's heart is in the right place—that is, has a love for all that is innocent and virtuous, and a deep abhorrence of everything opposite to these, she will not be very liable to form an erroneous judgment of any man who approaches her, no matter how many semblances of virtue he may put on. As for me, I do not pretend to have very acute perceptions, but from William Archer, you well know, I always shrunk with instinctive dislike."

"That arose, no doubt, from the estimate common report had caused you to form of his character."

"And are you prepared to doubt common report on this head?"

"Somewhat, I must confess. You have heard his solemn denial."

"Florence! I should think you had seen proofs enough. But, if not satisfied, a half hour's conversation with my mother will convince you that the writer of the letter you hold in your hand is quite as base as you had been led to believe him."

No reply was made. Florence folded the letter, and returned it to her pocket, with a deep sigh, breathed forth unconsciously.

Mrs. Hartley was deeply pained at observing this change in the mind of her young friend. But she said no more, trusting that the momentary weakness to which she was yielding would pass away, after conversing with her mother, who knew much more about Archer than the daughter wished to utter, or we to record.

CHAPTER III.

A SLIGHT MISUNDERSTANDING.

AFTER the conversation between Mrs. Hartley and Florence had taken a new direction, the subject of going to housekeeping was introduced. Like Mrs. Riston, Florence was in favour of the large house in Walnut Street, and urged Anna very strongly to change her mind, and let her husband take it.

"He is able enough," she said.

"Are you right sure?"

"He ought to be. Isn't he in the firm of R——, S——, & Co.?"

"As a junior partner only."

"He wished to take the house, you say?"

"At first he did."

"He ought to know better than any one else whether he could afford to do so or not."

"True. But he now thinks with me that it will be wiser for us to commence housekeeping in a style less imposing."

"I must say," returned Florence, "that Mr. Hartley

would have found very few women to object as you have done to a large and elegant house. I am sure the temptation would have been too much for me."

"If you had clearly seen that it was neither wise nor prudent to do so?"

"That might have altered **the case.** But I think few but yourself would have stopped to **consider** about wisdom and prudence."

"To their sorrow in the end, perhaps. I for one would much rather take an humble position in society, and rise, if good fortune attend me, gradually; than, after taking a high position, be, in a few years, thrust down."

"If there be danger of that, your course was doubtless best. But why should you apprehend any such disaster?"

"I do not apprehend evil; I only act, as I think, wisely. My husband is a young man who has been in business only for a few years. There are now but two of us, and we do not need a very large house. For both of these reasons it is plain to my mind that we ought to take our place in society without ostentation or lavish expenditure. It is barely possible that my husband may not find all his business expectations realized. I do not know what his prospects are, for I am in no way conversant with them. I only know that he had no capital of his own when he was taken into business. That he has told me. Now, if he should be very successful, it will be easy for us to go up higher in a few years. If not, and we had come out in costly style, it would be a hard trial and a mortifying one to come down."

"Your good sense is always guiding you aright," Florence could not help saying. "It is best, no doubt, that you should do as you have proposed; but there is not one in a hundred who would have exercised your prudent forethought; I am sure I could not have done it."

A few days after this Hartley and his wife decided to take the house in R—— Street. Then came the work of furnishing it. And here the prudent forethought of Anna was again seen. Her husband proposed to give up the whole business to a good cabinet-maker and an upholsterer, who should use their judgment and experience in such matters.

"As neither you nor I know much about these things, it will save us a world of trouble," he said.

Anna shook her head and smiled at this remark.

A shadow instantly flitted over the brow of Hartley. It disappeared as quickly as it came, but Anna saw it. The smile vanished from her lips, and her eyes filled with tears. She felt that, because she did not see in all things just as he did, he was annoyed.

"Am I self-willed? Do I differ with my husband from caprice?" were the self-examining questions of the young wife.

Hartley read her thoughts, and said quickly, in a voice of affection—

"You ought to know more about all these **matters** than I do, Anna; so you shall decide **what is best to do.**"

"I wish to decide nothing, **James.** I only wish to see and decide with you in everything. You don't know how much it pains me to differ: but ought I to yield passively to what you suggest if my own judgment does not approve? Ought we not to see eye to eye in all things?"

"We ought, certainly. But I have been so long in the habit of consulting my own judgment about everything, that I am, thus early in our married life, forgetting that now there are two of us to decide questions of mutual interest. I thank you for so gently bringing this to my mind, and for doing so in the very outset. Without thinking whether it would meet your views or not to become the mistress of a very elegant house, I decided to rent and fit up an establishment that I already **see** would have afforded more trouble than comfort. Your wise objections prevented the occurrence of that evil. Again I have decided to fit up the house we have taken in a certain way, and so decided without consulting you about it. Here is my second error, and you have, like a true wife, in the gentlest possible way, given me to see that I was wrong. I thank you for these two lessons, that had much better be given now than at some future time."

Hartley bent down and kissed the flushed cheek of his beautiful wife as he said this.

"And now, dear," he continued, "speak out freely all you have to say. As before, your judgment will, I doubt not, show that mine was altogether at fault."

"Do not talk so, James," returned Anna, her face covered with blushes. "I desire only to see with you and act with you."

"I know that, dear; but I am not perfect. I am, like all others, liable to err. And it is your duty when you clearly see me in error, to balance that error by declining to act passively with me. This I hope you will do."

Anna was humble-minded, and it pained her to hear such remarks from her husband, for whose moral and intellectual character she had the highest regard, while of herself she thought with meekness.

"Tell me, dear," Hartley said, after some time, "what is your objection to my plan of furnishing our house?"

"Mainly to the expense."

"Do you think it would cost more than if we attended to it ourselves?"

"It would, probably, cost double, and not be arranged more perfectly, so far as comfort and convenience are concerned, than if we were to do it ourselves."

"I don't understand how that could be."

"Your cabinet-maker and upholsterer would wish to

know if you wanted everything of the best; and you would assent. The best would be, no doubt in their estimation, the costliest. I saw a house once furnished in this way—a house not larger than the one we have taken. How much do you think it cost?"

"How much?"

"Nine hundred pounds."

"Indeed!"

"Yes. And I would agree to furnish a house with just as many comforts and conveniences on half the money."

Hartley's eyes were cast thoughtfully on the floor. It was some moments before anything more was said. The wife was first to speak. She did so in a timid, hesitating voice.

"Had we not better understand each other fully at once?" she said.

"By all means. The quicker we do **so** the better. Is there anything in which we do not fully understand each other?"

"Before we take another step, ought not I, as your wife, to know exactly how you stand with the world in a business and pecuniary relation? I feel that this is a very delicate subject for a wife to introduce. But can I know how to be governed in my desires if I do not know to what extent they can be safely gratified?"

"I trust there is no desire that you can entertain, dear Anna, that I am not able and willing to gratify."

THE MISUNDERSTANDING.
Page 97.

"That is altogether too vague," replied Mrs. Hartley, forcing a smile. "As your wife I shall regulate the expense of your household. I wish to do so wisely; and in order to this it is necessary for me to have some idea of your probable income."

"It ought to be between four and five hundred pounds a year; and will be, unless some unforeseen events transpire to affect our business."

Hartley seemed to say this with reluctance. And he did so really. The inquiry grated on his feelings. It seemed to him that Anna should have felt confidence enough in him to believe that he would not propose any expenditure of money beyond what was prudent. He would hardly have thought in this way if he had not actually proposed the very thing he tacitly condemned her for suspecting that he had done. He was not really so well established in the world as to be able to rent a house at a high rent, and furnish it in a costly style; nor even to give a *carte blanche* to a cabinet-maker and upholsterer to fit up, according to their ideas, the house he had decided to occupy.

The moment he allowed himself to think thus of his honest-minded wife, he felt an inward coldness toward her, which was perceived as quickly in her heart as it was felt in his.

Conscious that Anna thus perceived his feelings, and unable at the same time to rise above them, and think with generous approval of her motives, he did not, for some time, make any effort to lift her up from the unhappy state into which she had fallen. One unkind thought was the creator of others.

"What can she mean?" he allowed himself to ask. "Is it possible that she has imagined I was rich; and now, a doubt having crossed her mind, can she be trying to find out the exact state of my affairs? I never could have dreamed this!"

Both their eyes were cast upon the floor. They sat silent, with hearts heavily oppressed; he suffering accusation after accusation to flow into his mind, and lodge there; and she deeply distressed, from a consciousness of having been misunderstood in a matter that she felt to be of great importance, and which she had endeavoured to approach with the utmost delicacy.

Some minutes passed, when better feelings produced better thoughts in the mind of James Hartley. He saw that he had been ungenerous, even cruel in his suspicions. He imagined himself in her situation, and felt how deeply her heart must be wounded.

"She is right," he said inwardly, lifting his head, with the intention of saying that which should at once relieve Anna's mind. The first thing that met his eye was a tear falling upon her hand. His feelings reacted strongly. Drawing an arm quickly about her neck, he pressed her head against his bosom, and, bending over, murmured in her ear—

"I am not worthy of so good a wife as you, dear

Anna! What evil has possessed me, that I, who love you so truly, should be the one to make you unhappy? Surely I have been beside myself!"

Anna released herself quickly from the arm that had been thrown around her neck, and turned up to the eyes of her husband a tearful, serious but not unhappy face.

"Oh, James! dear James!" she said, in a low, earnest, eloquent voice. "Why do you speak so? I am only weak and foolish. It is enough that we love truly. If we find it a little difficult at first to understand each other fully, it is no great wonder. Love, true love, will in the end harmonize all differences, and make plain to each the other's heart. Let us be patient and forbearing."

"What you are; but I have much to learn, and you shall be my tutor."

Hartley again kissed his bride; but she looked serious.

"Not so," she returned. "It is to your intelligence that I am to look for guidance. I am to learn of you, not you of me."

"Never mind," was smilingly replied by Hartley. "We will reverse the order for a time, until my intelligence of domestic affairs is laid upon a truer basis than it seems now to be. But I think there will be no harm in our deferring all the matters now under consideration until to-morrow. Both of us will then be able to see more clearly, feel less acutely, and determine **more** wisely. Do you not think so?"

Anna gave **a** cheerful assent to this, and the subject of conversation was changed.

CHAPTER IV.

ALL RIGHT AGAIN.

CONSCIOUS that he had wronged Anna in thought as well as in feeling, Hartley's words, tones, and actions expressed towards her the tenderness that this **con**sciousness awoke in his bosom. By every little art **in** his power he strove to obliterate from her mind a recollection of what had passed.

As for Anna, she was grieved to find that her **well**meant, indeed her conscientious efforts, had been misunderstood. It would have been the easiest thing in the world for her to remain passive, and let her husband make all arrangements as his taste might dictate. But would this be right? **That** question she could not answer in the affirmative.

"He will think me self-willed," she said. "Twice already have I opposed his wishes, and how can he help feeling that I do this from an innate love of having things only my own way? Oh, if he but knew **my** heart! If he could see how gladly I would yield up everything to him if it would be right for me to do so!"

While Anna thought thus, her husband was experiencing the good results of her firmness. He was closely examining his own ends of action, and asking himself many questions, the answers to which enabled him to see the true nature of the ground upon which he was standing. In his heart he rendered his young wife full justice.

When next they recurred to the subject that had awakened a discordant string, it was seen in its true light by Hartley. He was the first to bring up the question about which there had been a difference of opinion,—felt much more strongly than expressed. This was on the succeeding day.

"I have been thinking a great deal about what took place yesterday," he began by saying in a serious voice.

Anna's heart gave a sudden bound. She looked earnestly at her husband. He could see that her lip slightly quivered.

"You are right and I am wrong," he continued; "all that concerns us should have our mutual consideration. As my wife, you ought to know exactly how I stand with the world, and I should not, through false pride, have any wish to conceal this from you. I have had many serious thoughts since yesterday, and to-day I feel that I am a wiser man. Will you forgive my ungenerous—"

"James!—dear James! I cannot hear you speak in this way," interposed Anna. "It is wrong for you to do so. Let what is past be forgotten. In the present let us live to good purpose; to the future let **us look** with hope."

"Very well. Let the past go with all its lights and shadows. To-day—that is, now—in the present time—we must act. What is our first duty?"

Anna made no reply.

"We have rented a house, and must furnish it."

Anna still remained silent.

"How shall it be done? I proposed one way; but it did not seem to you to be the right way, and like a true wife you said so, and gave an admirable **reason.** It was likely to involve a waste of money. You **suggested**, on the threshold of our married life, that we ought to understand each other fully. I have thought about that ever since. At first I could not bear **to** think of talking to you about the ordinary concerns of life—it seemed descending from **a** world of romance to a world of vulgar realities. Your intimation that you ought to know something about my pecuniary affairs, I confess, did jar upon my feelings; and I could not help showing it. But, Anna, you were right. How could you, as you truly said, govern your**self in** your desires, or regulate your expenditures, if you did not know how far I was able to meet them? It is right, then, that you should know precisely how I stand with the world; and in telling you the exact truth, I cannot but suffer a little from wounded pride— especially when the large house in Walnut Street comes up in my imagination. It is not to be concealed that I am not in a situation to rent such a house, and incur the heavy expenses that it would involve. I thought that I was, or rather imagined, without much thinking in the premises, that I was bound to make my wife the mistress of a very handsome house, with costly furniture, and all that appertained to an elegant establishment. But my wife had the good sense to undeceive me in this, and I thank her most sincerely for it!

"To come down to the main point, then, without further preliminaries, I am, as you know, a partner in the firm of R——, S——, & Co., one of the most flourishing houses in the city. But I am a junior partner, and entitled only to a certain dividend on the profits. This dividend, I have every reason to believe, will be between four and five hundred pounds. It may be less. I ought not to conceal from myself the fact, that a series of heavy losses would reduce my income much below the sum named;—still, I do not really apprehend anything of the kind. To all human appearance, our customers are some of the safest in the country. But it is the part of wisdom to exercise a prudent forethought."

Anna listened with deep attention. She did not reply, although her husband paused some moments to give her an opportunity for doing so.

"There is every prospect, however," Hartley resumed, "of my acquiring wealth rapidly. Our house has doubled its business in the last year, and if we go **on** increasing in the ratio that we have done for some time past, there will not be a richer firm in the city. My proportion of profit is to be increased to a fifth, at the expiration of five years from the time I was taken into the concern."

Hartley again paused; but Anna **still continued** silent.

"I have now told you all freely," he said.

"For which I thank you!" Anna replied in a serious voice. "I can now move forward without a feeling of insecurity. I shall **know** the ground upon which I tread."

"You will not, I hope, feel that there is any necessity for a very close economy?"

"All that either you or I want to make our condition as pleasant as would be desired, you are, I doubt not, fully able to afford. If there is no necessity for a very close economy, there is **as** little for a very free expenditure. Under all the circumstances, will it not be wise for us to **set** some limit to our wants?"

"In what way?"

"Determine how much, situated as we are, it should cost us in the year to live."

"I fully agree with you. Suppose, then, we say five hundred pounds."

Anna smiled.

"Too much or too little?" asked Hartley.

"Too much by at least two hundred pounds."

Hartley shook his head.

"We cannot live in a style that my business connections require that I should live in, on three hundred pounds a-year."

"I am not so sure of that. Three hundred pounds, if prudently expended, will go a great way. My father, I know, supported his family, and sent three of us to school for a number of years, on greatly less than that. And we lived as respectably then as we do now. We have rented a very good house. Let us furnish it well. After that is done, we shall find the lowest amount I have named quite sufficient for us. If not, it can be easily increased."

"Very true. I believe you see this whole matter in the best light. The furnishing of our house, as you have intimated, is now our first business. How and where shall we begin? As far as I am concerned, I know nothing at all about it."

"It is but little that I know;" replied Anna, "but there is one on whose experience I can safely rely—my mother. If you think it best, I will consult her."

"That will be the wisest course. A moment's reflection would have taught me this at first."

"My father has usually left all things relating to the internal economy of the family to her judgment."

"As I should leave all such things to yours," said Hartley, with a smile.

"No, no. Don't misunderstand me!" quickly replied Anna. "My mother, as far as I can recollect, never bought anything of importance without referring to my father. Her familiarity with domestic affairs enabled her to judge correctly in regard to what was needed; but his taste was consulted, and what he approved, I have noticed that my mother almost always selected. This set of chairs was bought about a year ago. I remember hearing mother say to father one day,—

"'If we can afford it, I think we should get a new set of chairs.'

"We were sitting in the parlour here when she said this. Father looked around and examined the chairs attentively for a little while.

"'They do look rather worn,' he answered, 'I did not notice it before. Our new carpets really shame them. By all means we must have another set.'

"The kind to be selected was then talked about. Mother proposed a plainer and cheaper style of chairs, but father thought they could afford a set like these, and mother acquiesced. On the next day they went together to a chairmaker's. I accompanied them. Four or five different patterns were shown; but mother made no choice, until she heard father express himself very much pleased with these. Without the slightest appearance of being governed by his taste, I saw that she inclined, gradually, to a choice of those my father had liked, and when she finally said which she liked best, it was done so delicately, that I am sure father did not suspect that his taste had guided hers. And yet it was so—or so appeared to me. I have witnessed the same deference to his taste frequently since. Now, just as my father leaves domestic affairs to my mother's judgment, do I wish that you would leave them to mine; and just as my mother consults my father's taste, do I wish to consult yours. Shall it not be so?"

"It shall!" was Hartley's instant reply, kissing, with warmth and tenderness, the sweet lips of his young wife, as he spoke.

CHAPTER V.

HOUSE FURNISHING.

On the next day Hartley, accompanied by Anna and her mother, started out to select furniture. It must be told that Anna did not defer to the taste of her husband quite so fully as she had represented her mother as doing to Mr. Lee. At the cabinet-maker's, there were several pieces of furniture that she induced him to purchase, notwithstanding he had expressed a decided preference for a different style of the same article. The reason may be easily guessed. A difference of, perhaps, five pounds in a sofa; as much more in a set of chairs, or a pair of pier tables, not any better for the additional price, but only a little more showy, was the only cause for this want of deference **to her** husband's taste on the part of Mrs. Hartley.

Sometimes the very natural desire to have things his own way, and the disposition felt to make a show, caused Hartley **to** feel chafed. But his good sense, aided by the experience he **had** gained since marriage, brought his mind back again to its **true balance.** He could not but approve the motives of **his** wife, and acknowledge that she was acting with prudence.

After their parlour, and a part of their chamber furniture, including carpets, had been selected, Hartley gave up all the rest into the hands of Anna.

In about two weeks the house was ready; the whole work of furnishing it having gone on under the direct supervision and instruction of Anna, aided by the wise counsel of her mother. When all was completed, the young couple took possession of their **new home.** Hartley was delighted with everything. The parlours were really beautiful.

"That sofa is much handsomer than I thought it was," he said, looking at it with pleasure. "It had a common appearance to me in Mr. ——'s wareroom."

"Because you saw it there in contrast with more showy ones," returned Anna. "I think it a real beauty, myself. I wouldn't ask a better one."

"Nor I, now that I can see what it really is. These chairs, too, are good enough for any one. I don't know that a neater pattern could be found. In fact, everything looks about two-hundred per cent better than I had any idea that it would."

"If we cannot be happy in a house furnished as well as this is, James, we cannot be happy anywhere," Anna said, leaning hard upon his arm, as she stood with her husband in the centre of their parlour, from which position they had been looking around them. "We want nothing for the sake of display; but only what will make us comfortable, and enable us to maintain that social position in which we can best act for the good of all around us."

As soon as Mrs. Hartley had commenced house-keeping, she was visited, as a thing of course, by all her friends. Some admired everything. Some approved the young wife's taste, and commended her prudence; while others wondered why she chose a particular article of furniture instead of another that was more fashionable, or why she did not get Saxony instead of Brussels carpeting for her parlours; and a great deal more of a like tenor. Among these friends was Mrs. Riston.

"Ah, my dear! So you have done as you threatened," said this lady, meeting Anna with a free air, and then looking around with a scrutinizing eye.

"Yes," was replied. "I have made a fair start in the world, and hope I shall be able to keep steadily on to the end with a clear conscience."

"It is more than many of us will do, then let me

tell you. Clear consciences are rare things in these days. But let me see what kind of a beginning you have made. These are your parlours."

The lady looked around for a while, and then shook her head.

"What is the matter? Are not things to your taste?"

"Not exactly."

"What do you see wrong?"

"Nothing that can just be called wrong; but much that is not at all in keeping with your husband's condition in life."

"I don't know about that. I think everything is in keeping."

"It is more than I do then. How much did you pay for your sofas?"

"Twenty pounds for the pair."

"I thought they were not above that price. What in the world possessed you to buy such common looking affairs? Or, did your husband think them quite good enough?"

The blood mounted to Mrs. Hartley's face, at this reflection upon her husband.

"No, they were my own choice," she quickly replied. "He liked a pair at forty pounds, and would have taken them if I had wished it."

Mrs. Riston shook her head.

"You are a silly child, Anna; but you will know

better after a while. It makes me downright angry with you every time I think about that splendid house in Walnut Street which you were foolish enough to refuse. Your husband is able enough to rent it."

"We both prefer to gain a little more experience than we have, before we dash out too boldly."

"If you don't dash out now, you will never do it. Take my word for that."

"No matter. Happiness in this life doesn't consist in dashing out. I, for one, shall be far happier in this quiet little nook, than I would be if I were mistress of a palace."

Mrs. Riston gave her head an incredulous toss, and said,—

"All that is well enough—very good talk. But I do not believe that you are so far superior to the rest of your sex as not to be captivated by elegance and splendour."

"I could have had a very elegant house and furniture of the most costly kind, if I had said but the word."

"And a great fool you were for not saying the word. You will repent of it one of these days."

Anna could not help smiling at her friend's earnestness.

"A rare display you would make, no doubt," she remarked, playfully.

"Wouldn't I! If I had the purse-strings I'd go to

housekeeping to-morrow. Then I'd show you style! I'd make my friends open their eyes."

Anna laughed outright.

"You may laugh. But I'd do it! Mr. Riston has been at me for the last three weeks about getting into a house of our own. I'm half inclined to say yes."

"Why don't you?"

"I think I will; but on one condition—that I have full liberty to choose a house and furnish it just as I please."

"Will Mr. Riston agree to that?"

"It's the only condition I'll give him a chance of agreeing to. If he makes a slave of me, I am determined to have a palace for my prison."

"Whether your husband can afford a palace or not?"

"Afford!" Mrs. Riston's lip curled. "I hate to hear a woman utter that word. Afford, indeed! I'll make him afford it."

The manner in which this was said sent a chill through Mrs. Hartley. She shrunk back, involuntarily, a pace or two from her visitor.

"But come," resumed Mrs. Riston, "let me see your chambers. There is nothing very wonderful here."

Anna led the way upstairs. Not a single article in the chambers met the lady's approval.

"Cheap—cheap—cheap," she said, glancing around. "Ah me! when will women get sense? Everything as plain as a pikestaff. Have you no taste, Mrs.

Hartley? No love for the beautiful? Has elegance no charm for your eyes?"

"No one can love external beautiful forms more truly than I do," Anna replied, seriously. "But, at the same time, I love moral beauties. When there is a just relation between the elegancies of life and the ability to possess these elegancies, the external beautiful forms are but the correspondents of moral beauties. But, if this correspondence does not exist, there can be no real enjoyment, no matter how beautiful the objects may be with which we are surrounded."

"All Greek to me, my dear! Give me the external beauties, and you may content yourself with the moralities, or whatever else you may choose to call them."

Anna made no further attempt to correct Mrs. Riston's false notions. She saw that it was useless. She permitted her to find fault with, and scold about everything in the house, and when she finally took her departure, bade her a smiling good morning.

CHAPTER VI.

A PRUDENT COURSE THE WISEST.

ONE day, some three or four weeks after Hartley had commenced housekeeping, a member of the firm of R——, S—— & Co. said to the senior partner,—

"I observe that James checked out, yesterday, three hundred pounds."

"Three hundred pounds!" Are you sure?"

"I am."

"Strange! what can he want with that sum of money?"

"You know he is married."

"Yes. But what has that to do with three hundred pounds?"

"He has gone to housekeeping."

"That explains it. He mentioned to me his intention of doing so some weeks ago."

"But don't you think he is pretty free with money?" A young man like him should not expect to dash out in very elegant style."

"True. But it is a question whether three hundred pounds will furnish a house very elegantly."

"Three hundred pounds will not go very far towards accomplishing that end, certainly. But it is more than probable that the major part of his furniture has been bought on a regular credit of six months, and that the three hundred pounds have been taken to pay for sundries not included in the bills for cabinet-ware and carpets."

"That may be. At any rate, it will be just as well for us to know all about this matter. Suppose you make some excuse to call in upon the young couple some evening this week, and see how they look."

"I will do so."

"Most sincerely do I hope that you will find all right.—That a just regard to James's situation in life will be apparent in everything around them. Too often it is the case, that, so soon as a young man is taken into business, he imagines his fortune made, and forthwith begins to spend money as freely as if it were water. Of this weakness I never should have suspected Hartley. But there is no telling what influence his wife, if she have a love of show and extravagance, may have over him. If any game of this kind is to be played, we will have to throw him over the wall the first chance that offers."

"Better, I think, to remonstrate with him first. If incorrigible, he will have to be cut off."

"All this, however, is assuming that he is running wild already. Let us be certain of this first. He has always showed himself a prudent young man."

"So he has. And it is hardly fair to suspect him too strongly upon the evidence we now have before us. Three hundred pounds may be for the whole expense of furnishing his house. If so, I do not think he has exceeded a prudent limit, when it is considered that his dividend on the profit ought to reach four or five hundred pounds per annum, as business now is."

As determined upon, one of the partners called in upon Hartley, and sat for half an hour with him, on the plea of a conference about some matter of business forgotten during the day.

"Did you see Hartley, last evening?" asked the other member of the firm, when they met next morning.

"Yes."

"Well? What was the result?"

"All right, I should think."

"I am glad to hear it. What is the appearance of things?"

"Elegant."

"Elegant?"

"Yes; but not too costly."

"How were the parlours furnished?"

"With admirable taste, considering the outlay, which could not have been extravagant."

"I am really gratified. Then the three hundred pounds must have been to meet the whole cost of their furniture?"

"Yes. If the rest of the house be in keeping with the parlours, which is no doubt the case, three hundred pounds is ample."

"I thought James had too much good sense to be led aside from prudence. Did you see his wife?"

"Yes."

"How did you like her?"

"Very much. I should call her a charming young creature."

"Is she handsome?"

"I think so."

"And a lady?"

"If she is not one, ladies are hard to find. Her face is very sweet; and, although she looks young, there is nothing childish about her."

"Who is she?"

"The daughter of old Mr. Lee, in the —— Insurance Company."

"Ah! Wasn't there a good deal of talk about her refusing a very advantageous offer some time ago?"

"Yes. She refused the hand of Gardiner."

"So she did. I remember now; and that I, in opposition to a good many lady friends, applauded her course. She is a sensible girl, I take it."

"So do I. Sensible for refusing Gardiner and accepting Hartley."

"Marriage usually makes or mars a young man's fortune," said the other. "I am happy to find that in our young friend's case, the former result is likely to occur. If he has a prudent, sensible wife, there need be no fear of him."

"That he has, I am ready to vouch," was confidently replied.

It was true, as Hartley's senior associates in business had supposed. Three hundred pounds paid all the bills that were made by Hartley in furnishing his house. Had he not been governed by his wife's better judgment in matters of domestic economy, the cost would have been nearly doubled. The way in which this would have affected his standing in the eyes of the principal members of his firm, the reader can easily guess.

Of all this careful observation of his conduct, Hartley had not the most remote suspicion. Had he married a woman whose love of display had seconded his desire to make an imposing appearance in the world, the first intimation of his error would have been, in all probability, a notice that he must curtail his expenses at least one-half, or leave the firm of which he was a partner. The mortification that this would have occasioned need not be described. So far from a fine house and costly furniture producing happiness, they would have made both himself and wife miserable.

CHAPTER VII.

A FOOLISH WIFE.

"I TELL you, Mr. Riston, it's no use to talk to me. As I have told you a hundred times before, I am not going to let you nor anybody else make a slave of me."

"But, Ellen, this is all folly. As a wife, you should be willing to discharge a wife's duties. You cannot expect your husband to be contented without having some place in the world that to him is really home."

"No doubt it would content his heart vastly to see

me drudging away from morning till night in the kitchen."

"Don't talk so like a silly woman, Ellen! You know better."

"I am silly enough in your eyes, no doubt. A woman is usually estimated by everybody else higher than she is by her husband."

"If so, it is easily explained," Mr. Riston said, in a slightly sarcastic tone.

"How is it explained?" asked the wife, with a look of defiance.

"Because he knows her best," was coolly replied.

"Mr. Riston, I won't allow anybody to insult me!"

"Nor will I, Ellen. If any one should insult you, let me know, and I will resent it on the instant."

"Your language and manner are insufferable, sir!"

"As is your unwife-like conduct, madam! I have borne with you until all patience is exhausted. I am sick to death of this way of living, and want to get into a house of my own. But you, from a selfish love of your own ease, refuse to perform the solemn pledges into which you entered at marriage. Your regard is all for yourself, and in no degree for your husband."

"And pray, sir," retorted Mrs. Riston with spirit, "in what direction turns your regard? Is it towards me, or towards yourself? Just to gratify your peculiar notions, you would make your wife a domestic slave. Is that so very unselfish? Humph! You had better take the beam out of your own eye, before you endeavour to get the mote out of mine."

"Ellen!" and Mr. Riston's voice was sterner, and his countenance darker than usual—"All this is the worst and vainest of trifling. For four years I have yielded to your pleasure in this matter. It has been a source of constant disturbance between us. I am resolved that it shall not remain so any longer. You may do as you like, but my course is determined. I shall go to house-keeping. If it does not suit you to become the mistress of my house, I shall hire a competent person, and confide to her the care of it."

"Oh dear!" Mrs. Riston laughed scornfully.

"Do not think, for a moment, that, in this matter, I am merely blustering," the husband said, with unusual seriousness. "It has taken me a long time to resolve upon this step. I have looked at the subject in every light. I have regarded your feelings and wishes up to the point where such a regard ceases to be a virtue. Now I feel that a woman who acts as you do, deserves not to be considered a moment by the man whom, in her marriage vows, she has cruelly deceived. I have already chosen a house."

"What!" Mrs. Riston started to her feet with a countenance deeply flushed.

"It is true, as I have told you," calmly replied her husband. "I have selected a house. If it does not meet your approval, I will defer to your wishes in the choice of one that does, if you think proper to join me in doing what I have told you it is my intention to do."

"*I* join you!" half shrieked the wife, with bitter contempt and defiance in her tones. "*I* join you, indeed! No! I will die before any man shall force me into this arbitrary measure. You have mistaken your woman, let me tell you."

"And you your man," was coldly returned.

A dead silence succeeded. The opposition and bickering of years had broken out at last into an open rupture. Mr. Riston's patience could hold out no longer against the selfishness of his wife, that did not permit her to regard his wishes or comforts in the least degree. Often before had he assumed an air of determination, in the hope that she would yield to his wishes, but with no good effect. Now, the determination was not assumed, but real. Mr. Riston had looked around him for a house, and had selected one with the fixed intention of renting and furnishing it, unless his wife should consent to go to housekeeping, and desire a different situation or style of house for a residence. The wife did not believe that he was in earnest; but in this she was mistaken. No good had resulted from yielding, on his part. He was at last resolved to use a different kind of influence.

Mrs. Riston, after the last remark of her husband, turned her back to him, and moved her chair so that her person would not fall within the range of his eye.

It was in the evening, and both sat moody and silent until bedtime. Mrs. Riston was indignant; and Mr. Riston firmly resolved to do what he had threatened.

On the next morning, before descending to breakfast, he said in a very calm voice,—they were the first words spoken to his wife since the previous evening :—

"Ellen, I wish you to consider all that I have said, as in earnest. I have the key of a house in N—— Street, through which I went yesterday. That house I shall rent, unless you choose another, and consent to go with me into it. I will not compel you to go into any house that you do not like; but, if you do not yourself select a house, I will take the one of which I have the key, and furnish it."

Mrs. Riston made no reply. She did not even look towards her husband.

"I will give you three days to make up your mind. After that, if you still decide to persevere in your present course, I shall certainly take mine; and the evil resulting from it must rest upon your own head."

The breakfast bell rang at the moment, and Mr. Riston left the chamber and descended to the dining-room. His wife remained behind, and did not make her appearance at table during the meal.

"My dear Mrs. Riston, how do you do? I am delighted to see you so early this morning. But how grave you look! What has happened, my dear?"

This was said by Mrs. Leslie, one of the lady's particular friends, **upon** whom Mrs. Riston called to communicate her troubles, as soon after breakfast **as she** thought **it** right to make a call.

"**Oh** dear, Mrs. Leslie! I am in a world of trouble **this** morning."

"What is the matter, dear?"

"Oh, that husband of mine, the perverse creature! has got into one of his tantrums again."

"Has he?"

"Indeed he has, and he seems worse than ever. He does lead me such a life!"

"What new crotchet is in his head?"

"New? **I wish** to goodness it was something new! But it's that old notion about housekeeping; and he is stark, staring mad about it."

"Oh dear!"

"I declare he worries the very life out of me, notwithstanding I have told him over and over again, that if he talked until doomsday about it I would not consent to become his slave. Go to housekeeping, indeed! I have seen too many women in that beautiful situation **to** wish to get into it myself."

"**If** your **mind is** made up about it, why give yourself so much trouble? It is only necessary to stand by your resolution, and **he** cannot help himself."

"So **I have** believed. But would you have thought it! he is actually going to **rent** a house and furnish it all himself."

"But he can't put you into it by bodily force."

"No; but he says he will hire a housekeeper to take charge of it if I don't go with him."

"Humph! That would be a pretty piece of business."

"Wouldn't it!"

"But you don't believe he is in earnest?"

"I am afraid he is. I never saw him in such a temper. I declare, his manner frightened me."

Mrs. Leslie did not know what to reply. While she sat with her eyes still upon the floor in a musing attitude, her friend resumed:—

"If he does really mean to push things to extremities, I shall have to give in, because I wouldn't have people think, for the world, that we did not live upon the most affectionate terms. I am too proud to have myself the town talk. But if he once gets the upper hand of me, there is no telling how far he may play the tyrant. That is the difficulty in the way, even after I have conquered my own will, which is no light task."

"Yes, that is to be well considered. If you give way an inch to some men, they will certainly exact the ell."

"And my husband is just one of those kind of men."

"You must yourself manage, if you do give an inch, to take three ells from somewhere else."

"That's it exactly, Mrs. Leslie! That is just what I have thought of doing. And it is to consult you about this that I have called in; but the first question to settle is, shall I yield?"

"I think you have taken already a very sensible view of that subject. You do not wish to be the town talk."

"No, I do not. I dread that only a little more than giving up to my husband, a thing that a woman of spirit never should do if it is possible to avoid it. If the matter could be kept between him and me alone, I would die before I would yield an inch; but in this movement he has completely out-generalled me."

"So it would seem, if he means really to do what he says. Suppose you let him go on a little further. If he does take a house and furnish it, you can become its mistress at the last pinch, and so avoid the exposure you dread."

"Yes, but look here, Mrs. Leslie. If I consent to go to housekeeping—if I give that one inch, I must have my three ells, you know. Now where are they to come from?"

"That is for you to determine."

"With the assistance of your advice?"

"It shall be freely given; but I want a small portion of ground to stand upon. Some clue to your wishes."

"Let me see," mused Mrs. Riston. "How shall I thwart him? How shall I get the complete upper hand? Where are the three ells to come from? Yes, I think I have it. He loves money, and hates to spend it; and I love it too, but only to spend it freely. If I go to housekeeping, I must have a splendid establishment."

"That's it, dear! put your hand deep into his pocket. If he will push matters so far—if the thing must be done, take care to have it done as you like."

"Trust me for that. He said if I didn't like the house he had taken, I was at liberty to choose one for myself."

"Did he? Then you have him."

"Haven't I? If I am to be a slave, I will choose a splendid captivity. He shall pay for it. Before a twelvemonth rolls around, if he isn't sick to death of housekeeping, I am no prophet."

Instead of wisely seeking to turn the current of Mrs. Riston's thoughts into a better channel, Mrs. Leslie encouraged her folly, and confirmed her in the mad resolution she had taken.

CHAPTER VIII.

A SAD PICTURE OF DOMESTIC LIFE.

Mr. Riston did not make his appearance at dinner-time, preferring to get something to eat at one of the public dining-rooms, to meeting his perverse-minded wife. He did not know that she was prepared to give him a much pleasanter reception than he had every reason to believe that she would.

Evening came, and the unhappy husband—for unhappy, though resolute, he really was—took his way homeward. When he entered his boarding-house, he went to the public parlour, and sat down there to await the ringing of the tea-bell, instead of going up to his own room. At the supper table he met his wife for the first time since morning. They sat side by side. But he did not speak to her, nor even look into her face. He was not a little surprised when she asked, in the ordinary indifferent tone with which she usually spoke to him, why he had not come home to dinner. He replied that he was very busy, and preferred dining in town. Mrs. Riston did not believe this of course. It was acting on his part as well as hers, and both understood that it was. But Mr. Riston felt puzzled.

After tea the husband and wife retired to their apartment. Mr. Riston made no attempt to introduce the subject about which they had jarred so heavily on the night before; but his wife dexterously brought it in, and then declared that, rather than there should be the exposure he threatened, she would submit, though with great reluctance. A few convenient tears watered this concession. Mr. Riston was softened.

"I cannot yield the point of going to housekeeping," he said. "But I am very willing to defer to your judgment in the selection of a house, and to let your taste govern in furnishing it."

"Where is the house you have fixed upon?" asked Mrs. Riston.

"In N—— Street."

"What kind of a house is it?"

"A very good house. I have no doubt but that you will like it. To-morrow we will walk round there. I have the key."

Mrs. Riston thought it just as well to reserve her objections until she saw the house, for then she could have something real upon which to ground them.

On the next day, after breakfast, in apparently a very good humour, the lady started out with her husband to visit the house he had pitched upon.

"How much is the rent?" she thought proper to ask on the way.

"Forty guineas," replied Mr. Riston.

"It can't be much of a house at that price," quietly remarked the lady.

"I think it a very excellent house. In some situations it would rent for sixty guineas."

Mrs. Riston said no more, but walked on. Her mind was made up as to the game she would play. In thinking how she would thwart her husband, she felt a secret delight. At length they were at the door. The key was applied, and they entered the house. First they looked through the parlours.

"These are very fine rooms," said the husband.

"Miserable paper!" said the wife.

"I don't know. I think it very good."

"Hardly fit for a garret. Isn't it astonishing that anybody could have the execrable taste to select such a pattern?"

"No doubt the landlord will give us new paper."

"And such mantel-pieces! I wouldn't be forced to look at them every day for a month if anybody would give me their weight in gold."

"I am sure, Ellen, that I don't see anything so offensive in them."

"Well, I do then; but come, let us go up into the chambers."

Up they went.

"Just as I supposed it would be. No paper on the walls."

"The landlord will paper the chambers, if we ask him, I am sure."

"He may paper them with gold leaf, if he chooses; but I would not live in his house."

"Why, Ellen! what do you mean?"

"Just what I have said. The fact is, I don't like the house at all, and can't imagine how you could have conceived, for a single moment, the idea of renting it."

"I think it a very excellent house."

"You do?"

"Certainly. A very genteel, comfortable house."

"Genteel! Oh, la! Your ideas of gentility and mine differ vastly. I can't live here, Mr. Riston. If

I must go to housekeeping, I will be the mistress of something that suits my taste much better than this does."

"Suppose you look for a house yourself. I am willing. If you are not pleased with this one, see if you cannot find another that you like better."

This was gaining one point. Mrs. Riston agreed to look out herself. Two days afterwards she said to her husband—

"I think I have met with a house that is just the thing."

"I am glad to hear it. Where is it situated?"

"In Arch Street."

"What is the rent?"

"Only a hundred and fifty pounds. It is a very cheap house for so fine a one."

"A hundred and fifty pounds!" exclaimed Mr. Riston in surprise.

"Yes, that is the rent."

"But you certainly do not think about our renting a house at that?"

"Why not? It is just the thing; I know you will be delighted with it."

"Not at a hundred and fifty pounds."

"The rent is very reasonable, Mr. Riston. You don't know what an elegant house it is."

"No doubt it is elegant enough, my dear; but we can't afford to pay such a rent."

"How much do you pay for your warehouse?"

"I pay a hundred and eighty pounds. But—"

"Very well; if you can pay a hundred and eighty pounds for a warehouse, I see no reason why you can't pay a hundred and fifty pounds for a dwelling."

"But a warehouse, Ellen, is a place of business; the rent of which is—"

"And a dwelling-house is a place of residence. Where is the difference, pray?"

"A very great difference. The rent of a warehouse always depends upon the amount of business that can be done—"

"Don't talk all that nonsense to me, Mr. Riston. I don't pretend to understand a word of it. To my mind there is no reason whatever why a man should pay more rent for a warehouse than for a dwelling."

"But look at it for a moment in a common sense—"

"I don't pretend to know anything about common sense, Mr. Riston."

"Really, Ellen, you are the most unreasonable woman I ever met in my life."

"Quite complimentary! No doubt you think so. But, thank goodness, your opinion of me will never break my heart!"

A pause in the coming tempest succeeded this fitful gust.

"You cannot be in earnest about the house you speak of in Arch Street?" at length resumed the husband.

"Why not, pray?"

"I cannot afford such a rent, Ellen."

"You don't suppose for a moment that I believe that kind of nonsense," retorted the wife.

"I tell you it is true!" Mr. Riston spoke with some warmth.

The lady tossed her head incredulously.

"As to paying a hundred and fifty pounds rent for a house, I can assure you at the threshold that the thing is not to be thought of for a moment."

"Well, just as you like. You can go and rent that pigeon-box in N—— Street if you please, and keep bachelor's hall. I shall not go into it, nor into any such mean concern. When I go to housekeeping, if go I must, it will be in a decent way."

"Decent! Pray what do you call decent?"

"I call the house in Arch Street a decent house."

Mr. Riston was angry and bewildered.

"It is no use for you to think of a house at a hundred and fifty pounds, Ellen," he said. "The thing is out of the question. My circumstances are not such as to—"

"There, there! now, Mr. Riston, I don't want another word about your circumstances! I have heard nothing else, I believe, since we were married."

"But won't you listen to common sense, woman?"

"Woman! Indeed!"

"Wife, then, if that will sound any better to your

ear, though a very strange kind of a wife you are. let me tell you!"

This remark would have made Mrs. Riston very angry if it had been uttered under different circumstances. But her mind was intent upon thwarting her husband, and she knew that she was chafing him severely. Considering his temperament, she was neither surprised nor pained at his words.

For two or three days the contention about the house in Arch Street went on. The husband remained so firm, that Mrs. Riston, after several conferences with her friend Mrs. Leslie, deemed it best to yield a little on the rent of the house, with the determination of making it up in the furniture. The handsome dwelling in Walnut Street, which Mr. Hartley had wished to take, still remained vacant. The rent of this was eighty guineas per annum. With much tact, Mrs. Riston directed the thoughts of her husband to this house, and actually induced him, by seeming herself to be resolved on the house in Arch Street, to propose to rent this one. With apparent great reluctance the lady yielded finally her preference for the house in Arch Street.

The contention with his wife about the choice of a dwelling had been such a severe one, that when a new difference of opinion in regard to the style of furnishing it showed itself, Mr. Riston retired at once from a combat in which he felt that inglorious defeat awaited him. With a sigh, and a foreboding of evil, he resigned to her the task of selecting the furniture, not, however, until he had expressed a willingness to remain where they were, rather than be subjected to the heavy expense which he saw too plainly housekeeping would involve.

"Oh, no, no," was his lady's reply. "This is all of your own seeking. Things have gone too far now. We have already taken the house, and my heart is set upon having it fitted up in a delightful way. I am not one of your changeables. When I once set my mind upon doing a thing, I must go to the end."

Nothing was left but quiet submission, or a prolonged contention, the result of which, in the husband's mind, was very doubtful. He weakly chose the former, against all the higher dictates of his reason; thus giving to a self-willed, vain, and unfeeling woman a new and more dangerous power over him.

CHAPTER IX.

FALSE FRIENDS.

WHILE the result of her contention with her husband was still doubtful, Mrs. Riston called upon none of her friends except Mrs. Leslie, who always encouraged her to do just what she wished to do, and whose advice was always such as to aid her in more effectually attaining her own ends. But no sooner was it settled that she was to become the mistress of an elegant house, than she was on the wing. Among the first persons on whom she called was Mrs. Hartley. She could not restrain the desire she felt to let Anna know that she was herself to occupy the beautiful house she had been so foolish as to pass by.

"I have news to tell you, my dear," she said, with a brightening face, after she had been seated a few minutes.

"Ah! What is it?"

"You wouldn't guess in a month."

"Perhaps not. I never was very good at guessing."

"I am going to house-keeping."

"What?"

"To house-keeping! Ain't you surprised?"

"I am truly. What in the world has caused you to change your views?"

"Circumstances. My husband set his mind so determinedly upon it, that nothing was left me but to consent. Would you believe it—the man actually set about renting a house and furnishing it himself, declaring that he would hire some one to keep it for him, and live there alone, if I did not choose to go with him? It's a fact! Did you ever hear of such a thing?"

Mrs. Hartley looked at her visitor in mute amazement.

"Well may you look surprised!" resumed **Mrs. Riston**. "But if I did consent in the end, after a hard struggle, to give up my freedom, it was only after stipulations honourable enough to my pride and ambition. He fought hard, **but** I conquered by perseverance."

It was impossible for Anna **to say a single** word in the pause that followed this sentence. **Her heart was** shocked. But of the real impression her communication had made, Mrs. Riston had no idea.

"My husband fixed upon a house very much like the one you have," the lady continued, "only something more genteel; but I told him *no* at once—that if I was forced to go to housekeeping, I must at least have a word to say in regard to the style in which I was to live. He yielded a little, and then I pushed him up hard, for I knew that nothing else would do. At first I insisted upon having a house in **Arch** Street at a hundred and fifty pounds rent."

"Mrs. Riston!"

"Indeed I did. He looked dumfounded. I urged, but he said *no*, with such **a** resolute air, and pled inability so very hard, that I abated a little. You remember the house in Walnut Street that you were so silly as to refuse when your husband wanted to rent it? Well that house still remained vacant, and I settled down upon it, determined not to descend a single step lower. My good man fought hard, but it was no

ANNA AND MRS. RISTON.

Page 139.

use. I was immoveable. At last he consented, and we have the keys. Ain't you sorry now that you did not secure it?"

"No," was the simple reply of Mrs. Hartley.

"You will be, then. Wait until I get it furnished. I'll dazzle your eyes for you. Mr. Riston has left all to my taste."

"Without regard to expense?"

"He tried to limit me to a certain sum, but I told him it was no use. We had no children, and therefore no particular reason for being over economical. Other people could live in handsome style who were no better off, and we had just as good a right to all the elegancies of life as anybody else. He preached about his not being able to bear the heavy expense; but I wouldn't listen to him a moment. I have heard about that ever since we were married. He would go to house-keeping, and now he shall have enough of it. Oh, but I'll show you style!"

Anna looked grave.

"What is the matter, my dear? Not envious, I hope, in anticipation?"

"No; Heaven knows that I am not!" Anna said, with a serious face and as serious a tone.

"What is the matter, then, child?"

"I am grieved at heart to hear any one speak of her husband as you are speaking, Mrs. Riston. Depend upon it you are wrong."

"Wrong for a woman to assert her rights and maintain them?"

"A woman has no rights independent of her husband."

"You are crazy, child! Must she be his passive slave?"

"No; nor should she attempt to play the tyrant over him."

"You do not mean to say that I attempt to play the tyrant over my husband?"

"Look closely into your own conduct, and answer that question for yourself, Mrs. Riston."

"I am not used to be spoken to in this way, madam!" An angry flush mounted to the brow of the visitor as she spoke, and a slight movement of the body showed that she was about to rise from her chair.

"Think, Mrs. Riston," replied Anna, "whether it would not be of use to you to know exactly what impression your words and conduct sometimes make upon the minds of disinterested friends."

"Ah! Well—perhaps it would. Please let me have the benefits of your impressions." This was said in a quick, sneering voice.

"Not while you feel as you do just now," Anna calmly said. "I have no unkindness in my heart towards you. I hope you will cherish none towards me. But I cannot help being affected as I am by your language. It gives me the most exquisite pain."

The manner in which this was said caused the angry feelings of Mrs. Riston to subside.

"You are a strange woman," Mrs. Hartley.

"I strive always to do right."

"So do I; that is, to have everything my own way, which I think the right way."

"Acting in that spirit, you will rarely be in the right," Anna firmly replied.

"Don't you think I am right in opposing my husband's penuriousness?"

"You should first be very sure that what you call penuriousness is not a just degree of prudence. What do you know of his affairs?"

"Nothing at all, except that he is very well off. As to the exact amount of his property, or how much he makes in a year, I don't concern myself. Of one thing I am very certain, my extravagance will never ruin him."

"I hope not. But you should not disregard his complaints, that you spend money too freely."

"I shouldn't regard it, you mean. But you can't judge of this, Anna. You don't know how constantly it has been rung in my ears ever since we were married."

"Perhaps this is your fault. Perhaps you have, from the first, been disposed to spend money more freely than you should."

"I differ with you; and I ought to know best." This was coldly spoken.

Anna felt that it would do no good to proceed, and the subject was dropped there. The visitor did not stay long. Mrs. Hartley had made her feel very uncomfortable.

CHAPTER X.

MARRIAGE CHANGES SOCIAL RELATIONS.

"HAVE you looked over the morning paper?" said Hartley to his wife, when he came home at dinner-time on the day the marriage of Archer and Florence had been publicly announced.

"Not particularly. Why?"

"A friend of yours is married." This was said without a smile.

"Ah! Who?"

"Florence Armitage."

"No!" Anna started, and looked serious.

"**It** is, I am sorry to say, too true; and she has married that young Archer."

"It cannot be so, James. Surely there must be some mistake."

"No. They went off together last night, and were married secretly. It is announced this morning in the papers. I am told that no one even suspected that they had met since the time their former engagement was broken."

"The girl must be insane!"

"How long is it since you saw her, Anna?"

"It is several weeks since she was here. Then she told me, as I mentioned to you at the time, that Archer had written to her, and that she felt inclined to believe public opinion judged him too severely."

"Which it has not done. He is just as bad as the general voice pronounces him; I believe worse. And this the poor girl will soon find to her sorrow."

"Did you hear at whose house the marriage took place? Or did they go to a minister's?"

"It is said that the ceremony was performed by an alderman at the residence of Mrs. Leslie."

"Now I understand. This is the work of that injudicious woman. Oh, what could she have been thinking about? She knew the character of Archer well."

"Few knew it better. But Mrs. Leslie is a thoughtless woman. Criminally thoughtless."

"I never felt any rational confidence in her, after I had known her for a short time. How much of evil such a woman can do, and yet move in the best society, and be well received there! Poor Florence! most sincerely do I commiserate her."

"How will her parents act? Do you think they will be so much incensed at her conduct as to refuse to receive her with her husband?"

"I think not. They will be grieved sorely. It will be a painful affliction. But they will not cast off their child."

"I am glad of that, for her sake."

"Yes; a consciousness of having acted wrong is grief enough, without anger and banishment added thereto."

"I suppose you will call and see her, and—"

"No, James; I do not intend calling upon her."

"Ah! why not? You were friends. She may have acted wrong, but she is still the same."

"Not to me. She is no longer Florence Armitage, but the wife of William Archer, whose character I detest."

"But shall you, because his character is vile, cease to regard the good that is in his wife?"

"No; I may regard all that is good in her still, but I cannot visit her. Would it be right for me to do it when I could not speak to her husband if he were standing by her side? I think not. Reverse the case. Would it be right for me to receive the visits of a lady who would not speak to you?"

"That question is not very hard to answer. I do not think it would. But no lady could have the good reason for avoiding me that you have for avoiding Archer."

"It matters not. Florence believes, no doubt, that her husband is innocent of the heinous sins laid to his charge, and therefore ought not to receive my visits while I treat him as if he were guilty. But more than this. I believe that no woman can love a bad man as her husband, and not suffer a moral perversion. This is another reason why I do not wish to be on terms of intimacy with the wife of Mr. Archer. And a still further reason is, that I ought not to visit freely in the family of a man so justly condemned by public opinion, lest he be thought one of my husband's friends."

"You would not feel bound to treat Florence coldly if she were to call upon you?"

"No; but I could not return her call. She has shown herself in this act so destitute of true womanly feeling, that I do not wish to number her among those I call my friends."

"All will not appreciate your motives. You will be thought harsh and censorious."

"I cannot help it. I desire the good opinion of every one, but not at the expense of my own self-respect. Florence has chosen her way in life; and it will, I fear, be a thorny one: but I cannot go along by her side, for I chose a different way."

"I hardly suppose that your visiting Florence occasionally would cause any one to think improperly of me," said Hartley.

"It *might* have that effect; and, while I live, no act of mine shall cast even a flitting shadow over my husband's good name or fortune."

Anna spoke with a generous warmth that caused Hartley's bosom to glow.

"I freely approve of what you say," he returned. "Florence has chosen her path in life, and that path cannot run side by side with yours. If you detest the husband's principles so fully that you cannot speak to him, you ought not to be on terms of friendly intercourse with his wife."

"No; I *feel* that I ought not; and *feeling*, you know, is sometimes a woman's strongest *reason*."

CHAPTER XI.

MRS. RISTON'S HOUSE-WARMING.

Mrs. Riston liked so little the plain way in which Anna spoke, that she did not again call to see her during the time she was engaged in purchasing furniture and fitting up her house. When all was ready, and she had taken possession, with more pride and triumph in her heart than a queen would feel in coming into her regal rights and honours, she did not forget Mrs. Hartley in her list of invitations to the splendid party she almost compelled her husband to consent that they should give.

This party did not cost less than three hundred pounds, and was, certainly, one of the most brilliant affairs of the kind that had been seen in P—— for a long time. Every room in the house, from the first to the third story, was decorated with hired or purchased ornaments, suited to the purpose, and all were thrown open to the company. At twelve o'clock a splendid supper was served to nearly three hundred persons, the table literally crowded with everything delicate and *recherche* that could be procured. The variety of confectionary displayed was wonderful; the wines were abundant, and the best and most costly that could be procured.

During the whole evening, Mrs. Riston moved among the company with the air and grace of a duchess. Her vanity led her to call the attention of almost every one with whom she conversed to this or that piece of furniture or ornament. She walked with her guests over the house, and listened with delight to their expressions of admiration. There were few present who did not flatter her vain heart, by approving all, and pronouncing her house the most perfect specimen they ever saw. One exception to this was Mrs. Hartley; but it must not be supposed that she was so unladylike in her deportment as not to call, even while talking with Mrs. Riston, everything around her beautiful, or as to appear cold and unapproving. She had too much delicacy of feeling for that. She had expected, when she left home, to find a house attired with unusual splendour. She did not think Mrs. Riston was right in indulging such an extravagant spirit, but, in her own house, and on a festive occasion, she had no right to show her disapproval.

But if she had no right to do this, she was not called upon to flatter a weak vain woman. As far as she believed it delicate for one lady to approve the tastes of another lady in the selection of her furniture, and in its arrangement, she did so, but without appearing to think that her guest wished her to be very profuse in her expressions of admiration.

Her manner, as may be supposed, did not please Mrs. Riston. To Mrs. Leslie, who was present, she said, with an ill-concealed sneer,—

"Mrs. Hartley is dying of envy. Have you met her?"

"No—not yet. I cannot come across her in this crowd."

"I have been by her side three or four times, and she praises everything, but in such a cold way! Any one can see that she is grieved to death for being such a fool as not to take this house when she could get it. What do you think she says about my gas chandeliers in the parlour?"

"I don't know, I am sure."

"She says they are *very neat!*"

"Oh, dear! They are *magnificent!*"

"So everybody says but her; and so does she say in her heart. I took her up into my chamber; but she only smiled a poor approval."

"She is a narrow-souled creature, Mrs. Riston. I always knew that. I almost wonder at your sending her an invitation."

"I don't think I should have done so, if I hadn't wished to mortify her."

"That you have done, it seems, effectually. She couldn't have dreamed of finding such a palace of a house as this. I must confess that, large as were my expectations, they fell far below the truth. But what does your dear, good, patient husband say to all this?"

"It will kill him, I am afraid. I have tumbled over him half a dozen times to-night, and it almost makes me laugh to see how sober he looks. I don't believe he has smiled since the company began to assemble!"

"Are you not afraid that this will attract attention?"

"Yes. It worries me terribly when I think of it; but then I remember that he has quite a long phiz at the best of times, and people know this. I wish, however, from my heart, that he wouldn't make such a fool of himself, and expose us to ridicule, as he certainly will."

"What did he say when he saw the style in which the house was furnished?"

"He actually stood aghast! Everything, you know, was left to my taste. I had most of the furniture in, and the house nearly ready before he could spare time from his business—that eternal business, business!—to look in upon my operations. When he saw the parlour, he turned pale. 'Ellen, are you mad?' he said. 'You know I can't afford this.'"

"Ha, ha!"

"'You would go to house-keeping,' I merely replied,

as coolly as you please. 'It is all your own doings. I told you over and over again that you would be killed at the outlay of money. But nothing would do. To house-keeping I must go—must become a domestic slave. I consented at last, and here, on the very threshold—before we even get into the house, you are fidgeting yourself to death about the expense. I am really ashamed of you.'"

"It will certainly be the death of him," laughed Mrs. Leslie. "But here he comes."

The object of their conversation came up at the moment, and Mrs. Riston glided away, leaving him with Mrs. Leslie. The lady noticed that, while he endeavoured to be cheerful, his mind was really depressed.

"You have a brilliant company here to-night," said Mrs. Leslie.

"Yes," and Mr. Riston forced a smile. "The gayest company I have seen for a long time. I hope you are enjoying yourself."

"Oh, yes! I always enjoy myself. I am one of your contented people."

"You are certainly fortunate in your temperament."

"So I have often thought. Let the world wag as it will, I always try to look at the bright side of things."

"I wish I could do the same."

"It is the easiest thing in the world. Good and

evil come in spite of us. If we will only enjoy the good, and not fret ourselves at, but patiently bear the evil, we shall get on smoothly enough."

The conversation was here interrupted by the presence of others. But Mrs. Leslie saw, or imagined that she saw, in the manner of Mr. Riston, a deeper feeling of uneasiness than what would arise from the contemplation of an extravagant waste of money, because he loved money.

It was nearly two o'clock when Mr. and Mrs. Hartley retired. As they rode away, both remained silent. Anna sighed once or twice.

"Foolish—foolish woman!" she ejaculated, after they had reached home.

"You may well say that! And foolish, foolish man, to permit such extravagance!" replied Hartley.

"He could not help it, I suppose."

"You mean that he weakly yielded everything to his wife's extravagance."

"Yes. And that was wrong."

"Wrong! It was criminal under all the circumstances. He is not able to waste money after this fashion. Few men in business are pressed harder than he is to make his payments. Scarcely a week passes that we do not have to lend him money. Still, I believe he would have been able to get over his present embarrassments, which are the result of two or three severe losses, had he not launched out into this extravagance. Now I have great fears for him. His situation is so well known among business men, that his credit will be shaken. He seemed conscious of this, I should think, for he looked wretched the whole evening —at least so it appeared to me. How he could feel otherwise, I cannot tell, when there were a dozen merchants present from whom he has to borrow money almost every day, and who, if they were to refuse to sell him goods, could make him a bankrupt in a month. If a single one of these withdraws his confidence, the alarm will be general, and poor Riston will fall to the ground like lead—"

"Ruined by his wife's extravagance,"—added Mrs. Hartley, finishing, significantly, the sentence uttered by her husband.

"Yes. That will be the truth. He now owes a large sum, and buys more or less every week, besides borrowing freely. I do not think it will be wise for us to let our account against him get much larger."

"O James! do not be the first to remove a stone from his tottering house, and thus throw it in ruins to the ground. Perhaps he may yet stand."

"That I do not wish to do. But if Mr. R—— had not been one of the company to-night, I should have felt bound to open my mind freely on the subject to him and Mr. S——. But R—— is a shrewd man of the world, and will not hesitate to speak and act for what he thinks the true interest of our business. I should not at all wonder if it were decided to-morrow to ask of Riston such prices for goods as would drive him away from our warehouse."

"O James!" said Mrs. Hartley, "is it not sad to think how easily a thoughtless wife may ruin a husband's credit, and thus destroy him? I never saw the danger before."

"I never thought of it much, until recently. Since you so wisely saved me from dashing out as I foolishly wished to do, I have opened my ears to remarks that hitherto made little or no impression upon me. I find that, where a man in business, whose capital is no larger than is needed safely and successfully to prosecute it begins to make a show in his style of living, he is looked at with some suspicion, and that remarks detrimental to his credit float about, and often affect him seriously. From some things casually said by Mr. R—— in my presence since we went to housekeeping, I feel well satisfied that if we had taken the house, since rented by Mr. Riston, and furnished it elegantly, it would have done me no good, and might, in the end, have led to a separation from the firm."

"Oh, no! Don't think so, James. I am sure that would not have taken place," said Anna, laying her hand upon her husband's forehead, and smoothing back his hair. This little act was only an effort to keep down the feelings that were struggling for expression and ready to gush forth.

"It is the truth, dear. You are my angel-guide, sent from heaven."

Anna's tears flowed freely. She could keep them back no longer.

"I will always seek to deserve your love and your confidence," she murmured, sinking into his arms. "You shall never find a single thorn in your path planted by my hand, if God will only endow me with wisdom to act well my part. But I tremble when I reflect, that I am liable, at almost every moment, through error of judgment, to go wrong."

"You will never go far wrong, Anna," was her husband's encouraging reply, "if you continue as you have begun, to seek for direction from above—if a religious principle be the life-germ of all your actions. For my own part I have no fears. Come what may, no disaster that visits me will ever be traced to your selfishnesss and folly."

"I pray Heaven that it may not!" was the wife's fervent answer.

CHAPTER XII.

HOW IT AFFECTED HER HUSBAND'S CREDIT.

Mr. Riston tried his best to entertain, as far as his personal attentions were concerned, the mass of people he had, jointly with his wife, invited to be witnesses of his folly. But he felt like a criminal all the evening.

There were more than a dozen persons present to whom he was largely indebted, and upon whose confidence and forbearance towards him depended everything. "How will all this affect them?" was a question constantly in his mind. When, at a late hour in the morning, he shook hands with the last departing guest, and returned to his still brilliantly lighted but deserted rooms, he threw himself upon a sofa with a heavily-drawn sigh.

"What ails you, man?" said his wife. "It won't kill you outright, I think. It is our first attempt at housekeeping, and we have opened handsomely."

"Have gone up like a rocket," returned the husband, in a tone of bitterness.

Mrs. Riston look at him with a slight curl of the lip.

"Soon to come down like the stick," he added, still more bitterly.

"You talk very strangely. What am I to understand by such language?"

"Why, that ten chances to one this brilliant party of yours—not mine—will ruin me."

"You are mad."

"I was mad, I confess, to let you make such a fool of yourself and me too. But I am sane enough now. I tried to tell you that I could not afford all this extravagant waste of money. But you shut your ears and would not hear me. You will both hear and feel before long. Your glory will be as short-lived as the early flower and the morning dew."

"You are raving, Mr. Riston!" said his wife, growing pale.

"I am not a man used to much extravagant speech. It would have been well for both of us, if you had made this discovery earlier; if you had believed me when I said I could not afford to spend money in certain ways proposed by you. I might as well have talked against the wind! But it is no use to upbraid you now—to throw your folly into your teeth. Necessity will do that soon enough; and Heaven grant that you may profit by the lesson you will receive."

"Mr. Riston, will you be kind enough to tell me what you mean—to speak out in plain and intelligible language?" This was said with an alarmed countenance, but in a steady voice; the wife looking fixedly at her husband. Her lips were firmly drawn together.

"The simplest language I can use is this," replied Mr. Riston, "and it is such as I have used over and over again without being heeded,—*I am not able to afford this style of living*, nor to give an extravagant party such as you have given to-night. What is the natural consequence which follows, when a man expends more than he can afford to spend? Of course he goes to the dogs, where I have now a very fair prospect of going, and that quite speedily. There were more than a dozen men here to-night, either of whom could make me a bankrupt **in a week.** It is only necessary **to raise** the cry **that** I am living beyond my means, which **is a** fact, **and** my credit is gone. Take that from me, **and** I am lost?"

"Credit! Have you nothing but credit?"

"Not much more, at present. I have lost a large amount by failures this year; and now my business is so clogged up that I am obliged to borrow large sums of money every day, in order to meet my payments. Destroy my credit, **and you** ruin me. That **even you** must see."

"But **it** is more than I can see, how this party or this house is going to destroy your credit."

"**A few** weeks will **probably** open your eyes," Mr. Riston said, in an angry voice; and, rising, he left the room, and went **up to his chamber.**

"All very fine," he muttered, glancing around. "But these are frost-work luxuries. They will soon **melt** away."

The presence during the evening of so many of the **very** men on whose estimation of his standing in business depended his safety, had set Mr. Riston to thinking seriously about the ultimate effects of the extravagant expenditures apparent to every eye. It was this that had sobered him so much during the evening. The more closely he thought about it, the more he felt alarmed.

The next **day** was one of Mr. Riston's hard days.

He had three heavy bills to meet, and four hundred pounds, borrowed money, to return. The thought of what was before him kept him awake during the greater part of the night. He would not have been so uneasy, had he not felt that, after the display he had made, the effort to borrow money would come with a bad grace.

Everything wore a very different aspect at the breakfast table on the morning that succeeded to the splendid entertainment. Mr. Riston sat in thoughtful silence, and tried to eat, but every mouthful was taken with an effort. Mrs. Riston was the picture of distress. The solemn earnestness of her husband, more than his words, had alarmed her. If his affairs should be at the crisis he said they were, it would be, she felt, a terrible stroke. What! To give up her splendid mansion! To shrink back into still deeper obscurity than that from which she had emerged! The thought alone almost drove her mad.

"You cannot be in earnest in what you told me last night, Mr. Riston," she said, unable to keep silence.

"If I was ever in earnest in my life, I am in earnest now," was replied. "I could have weathered through my difficulties, had I not insanely yielded to your miserable infatuation, and incurred all this expense, and what is worse, laid myself open to remarks and suspicions that will almost inevitably ruin me."

Mr. Riston spoke angrily. His wife made no answer;

but burst into tears, and rising from the table left the room.

The unhappy man sat musing for some time, and then withdrew from the breakfast room and passed the parlours, where he looked around in order to satisfy himself by a new observation, in regard to the impression that must have been made upon the minds of certain individuals who were in his thoughts. A sigh escaped him as he turned away and hurriedly left the house. It was nine o'clock when he reached the store. Two or three notes had arrived before him. One requested the return, on that day, of a hundred pounds, borrowed money, that he had not expected to be called on for in a week. The man who made this request had not been invited, with his wife, to the house-warming.

"But he has, no doubt, heard of it already," Mr. Riston said, mentally.

He opened another note. It contained the confectioner's bill. The amount was sixty pounds! Crushing this bill in his hand, he thrust it into his pocket, with a muttered execration against his wife, and turned to his desk to examine into his affairs for the day. A few hurried calculations made all plain. To his mind the aspect of things was appalling.

"If a breath of suspicion is whispered against me, I am gone!" he mentally said. "Nothing can save me. In a few weeks, if I can retain the confidence of every one, I shall be safely past the crisis of my affairs, and on smooth water again. But can I retain it? Alas! I fear not. Confound this housekeeping folly, and this party! They will prove my ruin!!"

But idle fears and vain regrets would accomplish nothing. There must be action, and prompt action. As early as half-past ten o'clock the merchant was on foot.

"Good morning, Riston!" said the first man on whom he called, extending his hand as the money-seeker entered his store. "Really! that was a magnificent affair of yours last night. I have never in my life been present at a more splendid entertainment. And what a lovely house you have got. What rent do you pay?"

"Eighty guineas."

The other shrugged his shoulders.

"Rather high, I must confess," Riston said. "But we have no children, and my wife must have something to see after. We can live in handsome style, and not be at a very heavy expense."

"True, that does make a difference. Children, especially half-grown daughters, are a great expense. Mine, I know, are terribly hard on money. But that party must have cost you three hundred pounds, Riston."

"Nonsense! It didn't cost one-fourth of it."

Riston was far from suspecting how near the bill would amount to the sum mentioned.

"If you get off with less than three hundred pounds,

you may think yourself a fortunate man. Why, your confectioner's bill will be sixty pounds, at least."

"How do you know?" asked Riston, with surprise.

"I heard it, somewhere, yesterday. I believe it came from your wife."

"My wife, to speak the truth, is a little too fond of making a display. To please her, I consented to give a party, and as I had enough of business matters to occupy my time, I left all the arrangements with her. I must own that she astonished me with the result of her preparations. Sixty pounds for confectionery! That will never, never do."

"I heard, also, and I believe it came from as authentic a source, that your wines cost nearly as much."

"Impossible! They did not cost one-half of that sum."

"My wife saw Mrs. Riston only the day before yesterday, and had it from her own lips."

Riston was confounded. It seemed that his wife had not only indulged the most lavish expenditure, but had actually blazoned it about. It was impossible for him to ask this man to lend him money. He could not have looked him steadily in the face while he made such a request. As quickly as he could, he withdrew, and called upon another business friend. Here he was met by remarks of a similar kind, though made with rather more delicacy. Before leaving, he ventured to put the question—

"Can you spare me anything to-day?"

"Nothing at all," was replied. "We have a large amount ourselves to pay."

The same allusions to the splendid party he had given met poor Riston, go where he would. He found it almost impossible to borrow money: everybody would have been happy to accommodate him, but nobody had anything to spare. At one o'clock he returned to his warehouse, without having accomplished, comparatively, anything at all. He had gone the entire round and could get no adequate assistance. Every one congratulated him on his brilliant entertainment and splendid house, but few had any money to lend him. Even those who had been most willing before to assist him, were now reserved, and, professedly, unable to do anything.

"I am a ruined man!" he said to himself, bitterly, as he sat down to collect his thoughts. "As I feared, this last act of folly has decided my fate."

In the hope of sustaining himself by a heavy sacrifice, until he could get over his accumulated difficulties, Riston went, as a last resort, to a money broker, and offered him three per cent. a month, besides a liberal commission, if he would get him the amount he wanted on his own note of hand, at four months. The broker promised to do his best, but was not sanguine. Three o'clock came; nothing had yet been done. Half-past three—the broker was not in his office Riston was unable to compose himself sufficiently to sit down and wait for him,—he walked the floor with agitated steps for ten minutes.

"All is lost!" he ejaculated, stopping suddenly and looking up at the clock—the time had passed on until it lacked but a quarter to four.

"Even if I had the money now, there would scarcely be time to lift the notes. Fool! fool that I was, not to have gone to the holders of them, and endeavoured to make some arrangement. It would have been less disastrous than to have my paper dishonoured."

While thinking thus the broker entered quickly. Riston looked eagerly in his face. Hope died instantly.

"I can do nothing for you," said the agent in a voice of regret; "money is very tight."

Without a reply, Riston took the note he had placed in the broker's hands, put it into his pocket, and thanking him for the trouble he had taken, retired. He felt, to his own surprise, perfectly calm. The great struggle had ceased—the end had come. He yielded passively to the current, and let it bear him down. Returning to his warehouse, he informed his principal clerk, in a few words, of the state of his affairs; and then gave directions to have all the books settled up with the utmost despatch, previous to a meeting of creditors, which he should call at the earliest possible day, that a full exhibit of his business could be made. He then took his way homeward. As he walked along, with his eyes upon the ground, he thought of his wife—not with anger, but with pity. It was his intention to inform her fully of what had occurred, and to make her see clearly that her extravagance had been the cause of his ruin. He knew that this must produce acute pain; but it would, he trusted, be salutary.

CHAPTER XIII.

TAKING A LOWER PLACE IN SOCIETY.

For some time after her husband went out, Mrs. Riston suffered great distress of mind. The thought of having to give up her splendid house was almost as terrible as the thought of death. If her husband should really fail in business, she felt that she could not survive the mortification.

"But I don't believe a word of it," she roused herself by saying. "This is only a bug-bear that he has conjured up to frighten me."

In spite of her effort to believe this she could not help feeling uneasy. About twelve o'clock visitors began to drop in. Mrs. Riston was occupied with these for two or three hours. All with flattering words ministered to her vanity, and caused her to feel how intimately blended with her happiness were the elegancies with which she was surrounded. Ever and

THE WIFE.

anon the thought of **what** her husband had said would **pass through** her mind, and produce the most acute pain.

At length she was alone again. It was past four o'clock, the hour for dining, but Mr. Riston had not yet returned. She dreaded to see him come in, and yet felt anxious about his prolonged absence, **for** it did not seem a precursor of good. The clock **was** striking five when she heard his footsteps in the hall. He went into the parlour, but remained there only **a** moment. She next heard him ascending the stairs with a more deliberate step than usual. She looked up into his face with an anxious and inquiring eye as he entered the chamber where she was sitting. Its expression startled her. There was something about it that she could not understand. She was not long in suspense.

"The worst has come to the worst, Ellen," he said, **in** a calm, cold voice, taking a chair by her side, and looking fixedly at her. "As I feared it would be, so it has turned out. I could hear of nothing, go where I would, but the splendid party, and the amount it must have, or really did cost; but nobody had any money to lend. Men who trusted me freely last week, and **even** yesterday, and who could have done it as easily to-day, had nothing to spare. From ten o'clock until four I strove, with all the power I possessed, to get the amount of money needed to **keep** me from bankruptcy, but in vain. I am now a dishonoured and broken merchant."

A cry of anguish burst from the lips of his unhappy wife as he said this.

"**I do** not upbraid you as the cause of my misfortune," he resumed, as soon as the excitement of Mrs. Riston's feelings had in some measure subsided. "That would avail nothing. But it **is** only right for you to know that but for this house, and the style in which it is furnished, and the extravagant display made last night, my credit would have remained untarnished. The money needed to meet my payments to-day **would** have been easily procured, and in a few weeks my feet would have been on firm ground again. As it is, **I** shall have to give up all to my creditors, who **will** place my effects in the hands of trustees. **Forced** settlements will involve sacrifices, and the end will be that I shall turn out an insolvent debtor, and be thrown penniless upon the world to begin life again."

Mrs. Riston was stunned so much by this announcement that she could not speak. Her face was pale as ashes, her hands clenched, and her eyes fixed like one in a spasm. So paralyzed was she that she had to be carried to bed, scarcely sensible of anything that was passing around her.

A downward tendency is always rapid. Mr. Riston called a meeting of his creditors, and submitted, in a manly spirit, a statement of his affairs. Trustees were appointed, and all his effects placed in their hands. His elegant furniture was sold at public sale, within three weeks of the date of its purchase, and the cabinet-maker, upholsterer, and others, as well as the wine-merchant and confectioner, were compelled to await some ten or twelve months before receiving their final dividend on the bankrupt's assets.

Mrs. Riston retired to an obscure boarding house, in the upper part of the city, in ten days after she had taken possession of her palace, as she had called it, with such lofty feelings. She retired a broken-spirited woman. Her husband's conduct in the trying ordeal through which he was compelled to pass, gained him the respect and regard of many who were ready to assist him. He resumed business, after the lapse of two months, in a small way, and commenced again his upward struggle, fully resolved that his wife should never again have any control over him that was not the control of reason.

"If I feel able at any future time to go to house-keeping in a quiet, economical way, I shall not regard her objections," he said to himself, while thinking over his plans for the future. "She will have to be governed by my wishes now. I have yielded to hers long enough. I am willing to devote myself to business early and late, and to take upon myself all its attendant cares and anxieties for our mutual good. It is but right that she should fill the domestic sphere as fully as I do that of business. Had I insisted upon her doing so at first, her mind would never have become warped, nor her desires so extravagant. I might still have retained my good name,—have still **been** engaged in a prosperous business. But the time past shall suffice. My clear convictions of right shall **never yield** one iota to her whims, passions, or caprices."

Riston was as good as his word. He held, so to speak, a tight reign on his wife ever after. She, it must be said, was a more passive subject than before, and yielded to his wishes much easier. But she was not happy. She hardly ever went out, and scarcely any of her old friends cared about retaining her acquaintance. At home, she drooped about, and went through whatever domestic duties she had to perform, as if she were an automaton. She had no genuine love for her husband, and he felt **it.** Their meetings were cold, and their intercourse limited **to** a few commonplace remarks, **or** questions and answers necessary to be made. Thus passed their days, neither of them caring how soon the time came for separation.

CHAPTER XIV.
TRUE LOVE TRIED AND PROVED.

In presenting a contrast to the wise and prudent conduct of Mrs. Hartley, we have kept our leading character in the background for some time. We have **done so** for two reasons,—in order to present the contrast; and, because we did not think it possible to give picture after picture of the quiet life of Mr. and Mrs. Hartley and preserve sufficient interest to compensate the reader. Anna, it has been seen, acted in the very commencement of her married life with an unselfish regard to the good of her husband. She could have yielded passively to his wishes and become the mistress of an elegant house; and she had temptations to do so that few women so situated would have thought of resisting. But she did not love her husband blindly nor selfishly, but wisely. She thought of her duty as a wife, and manifested the quality of her love by the right performance of her duties from the first day of her marriage.

But it was not alone in a due regard to external things that Anna manifested the quality of her love. She sought to regulate the affections of her mind, and bring them into due subordination to the highest and purest principles. Her husband had his weaknesses, as have all men; his prejudices and his passions. And she was not free from imperfections. Reason told her, that if evil overcame evil in a contention between husband and wife, victory would be as destructive to happiness as defeat. But that if evil were overcome of good, both the victor and the vanquished would be wiser and better, and therefore happier for the contest.

In acting from this clear sense of right, Anna had

many hard contentions with herself. When anything like an arbitrary, self-willed, or unamiable trait in her husband's character presented itself, her heart felt wounded, or inclined to meet self-will with self-will, or arbitrary words and conduct with stern opposition. But reflection, and a struggle with herself for the mastery over the tendencies of a naturally evil heart, would soon make her vision clear, and her mind calm. And then she could act the wife's true part well and wisely.

Hartley was not so blind but that he could see all this in Anna. It made him feel humble in spirit, when, after some slight difference, in which he had spoken with a warmth bordering on unkindness, she would answer in gentle terms, that were redolent of a sweet forbearing spirit; or, when he had opposed his wishes to hers, she would yield to his desires with a cheerful grace, that rebuked his own eager selfishness. He saw that, in every contention, she gained the real victory, even though he, in appearance, carried the point at issue.

"God bless her!" he ejaculated fervently, as he left his house one morning, the tears coming to his eyes. "She is an angel! She saves me from myself. I never dreamed that I was so self-willed, so unamiable, so much in the love of dominion as I am, until she caused me to see my own heart clearly reflected from the bright, pure surface of her own. I can understand now how a wife's character elevates or depresses that of her husband. Had she been different; had she been self-willed, even as self-willed as I am; had she been fond of dress, or display, or admiration;—had she been, in fact, anything but what she is, a loving, almost faultless, wife, I tremble to think of the unhappy influence she would have had upon me. I did not know that I had so many faults of character as I have; faults that a selfish wife would have confirmed, but which my own dear Anna helps me to remove at the same time that she does not appear to see them. God bless her! I say again."

This warmly-uttered tribute to the virtues of his wife was occasioned by some one of the many instances of forbearance which Mrs. Hartley was compelled to exercise towards her husband, who, excellent as he was, had his weak points, his faults and his foibles. But her manner towards him was always so gentle and kind, that it reproved him the instant he was betrayed into any act or word that was calculated to wound or disturb her.

They had been married for six months. During that time all external circumstances had conspired to make their life happy. The business prospects of Hartley were more flattering than at first. Trade was brisk, and sales heavier than usual. No wonder that they could live in sunshine, with but few light clouds to flit over their sky. But a change came. Let us see how it affects them.

When Hartley reached the warehouse on the morning just referred to, he found both of his partners greatly disturbed in mind. On inquiring the cause, he learned that letters had just come to hand with the intelligence of three heavy failures in C—— of houses indebted to the firm to a very large amount.

The effect of this disaster upon their business, Hartley at once saw. The same firm was also largely indebted to several houses in P——, whose condition was not thought to be sound, and those houses in turn were debtors to R——, S——, & Co. in heavy amounts. Should the failures prove as bad as the first intelligence represented them to be, it was a matter of great doubt as to the ultimate consequences. R—— was particularly dispirited, and S——, a man of much stronger nerves, was a good deal agitated.

"Bad, very bad, James," the latter said to Hartley. "I am afraid it will break us up."

The young man turned pale.

"Oh, no! Hardly so bad as that, Mr. S——?" he replied in a husky voice.

"There is no telling. We shall be crippled without doubt. There is a fair prospect of our losing ten or twelve thousand pounds by these failures. I need not tell you that such a loss will shake us to the foundation. I must own, that I am deeply anxious about the consequences."

The heart of the young man sunk. To him, even if

the house stood firm, the effect would be severe. If ten thousand pounds were lost, or even one-half that sum, it would reduce to a very small amount his dividend of the profits, if it left him anything at all. His first thought was of his wife, and, as her image arose in his mind, a pang went through his breast.

During the morning, a hundred floating rumours assailed the ears of Hartley and his associates in business, none of them at all encouraging. The whole prospect was dark. Every one who had debtors in C—— was alarmed. A dozen merchants there were talked of as affected by the failures that had already taken place, and in danger of suspending. Several of these were also customers of R——, S——, & Co. who held their paper to considerable amounts.

In this state of anxious uncertainty the hours passed on until it was time for Hartley to go home. He shrunk from the thought of meeting his wife. It was impossible for him to conceal what he felt; her quick eye would read the change in his feelings the moment he came in.

With an effort to appear as cheerful and free from concern as usual, Hartley came into the presence of his wife at dinner-time.

"James! What is the matter?" she exclaimed, the moment her eye rested upon his face. "Are you not well?"

His effort to put on the appearance of a quiet mind

had proved vain. He had never practised simulation, and could not do it now. The eager questions of Anna, and her alarmed face, caused his own countenance to assume an expression of deep distress.

"O James! What has happened?"

"Sit down, love, and I will tell you all. **But do not be alarmed. It** may not be as **bad** as we fear."

Hartley said **this in a voice** meant to quiet the anxiety of his wife. But she grew deadly pale.

"My father—" she could but faintly utter.

"Oh, no, no! Nothing of that," replied Hartley, comprehending the nature **of** her thoughts. "Your father and mother, and all belonging to them are well. I allude to my business affairs, which have suddenly assumed a threatening aspect."

"Is that all?" murmured Anna in **a** faint **voice,** sinking into her husband's arms. "I feared that something dreadful had happened."

For an instant Hartley felt vexed at the indifference shown by his wife in a matter that went to his very heart. But the relief this seeming indifference afforded his own mind was so great, that he began to feel half-ashamed of himself for discovering so much agitation.

"That is all," **he** returned, after a short silence, in a calm voice. "But to me it is a very serious matter."

"And if to you, is it not the same to me?" quickly replied Anna, perceiving in a moment the impression her remark had made. "Vague fears were instantly excited by your looks and words, and they always create a paralyzed condition of mind. But tell me, dear husband, what has happened? No matter what it is—no matter how it affects us externally, it shall find your wife unchanged. She will stand firmly by your side, if all the world forsake you. Speak to me freely. Do not fear for me. Am I not your wife?"

"Yes—you are truly my wife—my angel-wife—my guide, my companion, my comforter. Feeling now how rich I am in possessing the love of a true heart like yours, it hardly seems possible that a little while ago, with the danger of the ruin of our house by heavy failures looking me in the face, my spirits could have been so prostrated. But it was of you that I thought. I trembled at the prospect of a change that would affect you."

"Think not of me. Fear not for me. Come what will, if I retain your love and your confidence, I shall be happy. But what has happened, James? Don't hesitate to tell me all."

Hartley briefly related what the reader already knows in regard to the certain and probable losses that would be sustained by the failures.

"What the effect will be," he said, in conclusion, "cannot now be told. It may force us to close up our business and dissolve the firm. Most certainly it will reduce my income for the next year very low, if not cut it off altogether."

In uttering the last sentence, Hartley's voice trembled.

"My dear husband," quickly replied Anna, with a smile, and speaking in a calm tone of voice, "you believe in an overruling Providence; and you know that whatever befalls us here is of divine permission, and intended for our good."

"I know it, Anna, but it is hard to feel that it is so."

"And yet it is so. We know it is so. This is faith; but faith that is only in the understanding is nothing. The heart must give its affirmation as well as the thought. Let our hearts do this. We believe the threatened events, if they do take place, will be wisely ordered or permitted for our spiritual good. On this rock let us plant our feet, and the waters may rage around us in vain. Think, for a moment; if reverses are necessary, in order that our minds may be opened more interiorly towards heaven, through trials and changes in our external lives, would you, if you had your choice, and your thoughts were clear and calm, hesitate to choose the rougher way in life? James, I am sure you would not! What is our brief day here, compared to an eternal state hereafter? This is the way for us to think and feel."

"True, Anna; still it is hard, very hard, for me to feel as well as think so wisely. If my thoughts *were* clear and calm, and the choice were presented, I believe

I would choose the better part. But the great difficulty is to keep off doubt and fear, that cloud and disturb the mind. If I could see it all as clear as I now do, it would be easy enough. But the moment I direct my mind to the circumstances that surround me, and see the ruin of all my worldly prospects staring me in the face, I cannot help trembling. I am no longer looking up, but downward."

"Let it, then, be my task to point your eyes upward. You, mingling in the busy strife of men, and surrounded by the sphere of business, with its anxiety and care, and fears of the loss of worldly goods and worldly honours, must, necessarily, be influenced by the quality of this sphere, and have your mind affected with like anxieties, and cares, and fears. But I live in another sphere. I cannot be affected, daily, as you are. I can look up with a steadier eye. Mine, then, shall be the duty of holding up your hands. When cares oppress you, come to me, and I will show you how vain they are; if anxious, lean upon me, and I will give you to feel that no one need be anxious, while the Lord rules in heaven and earth. If we must take a lower position in life, I will take it with you, and encourage you, if you fear, in descending."

As Mrs. Hartley spoke, with a warmly eloquent voice, her face beamed in beauty that was not of the earth, earthy. In the eyes of her husband, she had always borne a lovely countenance, but she was lovelier now than ever. Clasping her with tender earnestness in his arms, he said,—

"May Heaven shower upon you its choicest blessings! You make me ashamed of my own weakness; of my own want of trust in the Providence that I know governs all things well. With you by my side, life's journey can never be a very painful one; for you will make for me all the rough places of peevish nature even. Come what will, whether prosperity or adversity, I shall ever find your heart as true to love as is the needle to the pole."

"Yes, ever," was the low, murmured reply.

CHAPTER XV.

A CHANGE.

HARTLEY returned to the warehouse after dinner, feeling much more as a man should feel, under circumstances of trial, than he did in the morning. The afternoon brought further intelligence from the west. It was decisive. The houses that had suspended payment would each make a most disastrous failure, and it was almost certain would carry two others with them, both of which were indebted to R——, S——, & Co.

When Hartley came home at night, his mind was again overshadowed. Anna had suffered a good deal during the afternoon, for her husband's sake. She could enter into and understand his feelings, and she therefore knew how hard a trial he had to bear in the threatened ruin of his bright hopes of worldly success. Nor was she indifferent, so far as herself was concerned. To all, prosperity and the temporal blessings it brings, is pleasant. And Mrs. Hartley could enjoy them as well as others. It was not, therefore, without an earnest struggle with herself, that she could rise, really, into that state of composure and trust in Providence, that she had so strongly urged upon her husband. When he came in, at the close of the day, she saw that he was again depressed in spirits; and again she sought to raise his thoughts above the mere fact of present temporal losses, to a realization of the truth that all things are made, in the divine Providence, to work together for good. In this as before, she was successful, even though more recent intelligence than that received in the morning tended to confirm Hartley's worst fears.

On the day following things looked still more gloomy. A week elapsed, and all yet remained dark and threatening. A month passed, and the house of R——, S——, & Co., considered one of the most promising in the city, suspended payment, and commenced winding up its business. There was property enough to pay off all the debts, and leave something over. But as Hartley had put in no capital, and all the profits and more than half of the capital had been lost, he went out of the concern with less than fifty pounds in his pocket, the two senior partners remaining to close up everything. Requiring the services of some one, R—— & S—— offered Hartley a salary of a hundred and fifty pounds, which he gladly accepted, and from a merchant with large expectations, fell back into his former capacity of a clerk. It required all the young man's philosophy, aided by the hopeful, trusting spirit of his wife, to bear up with anything like fortitude. For the sake of her who was loved beyond what words could express, he grieved more deeply over this reverse than he would have done had he stood alone in the world. She would have to bear half of the burden, and the thought of this touched him to the quick.

As soon as Anna knew that her husband had dissolved all connection with the house in which he had been a partner, and that his income was fixed at a hundred and fifty pounds per annum, she said to him with a cheerful face and tone,—

"We must look out for another house, James; the rent of this one is too high for us now."

"I don't know, Anna; I think I can still manage to pay the rent. I have partly engaged to post a set of books, which I can do by devoting a couple of hours to it every evening. If I will undertake them, it will increase my income nearly thirty pounds. I would rather do it than move. I can't bear the thought of that.

We live so comfortably and genteelly here. It will be impossible to get a house that is respectable, for a **rent** low enough to make it an object to give up this one."

"So far as mere appearance is concerned, James," replied his wife, "I do not think we should consider that. What is right for us to do? That should be the question. Is it right to live up close to our income?"

"I think not," Hartley could not help replying.

"Can you, after being closely engaged all day, post books for two or three hours every evening, without affecting your health?" pursued Anna.

"I can hardly tell."

"Is it not reasonable to conclude that such incessant application would be injurious? I think so. How much better would it be to get a smaller house farther from the centre of the city, and reduce all our expenses to the lowest scale. If good fortune again smile upon us, **we can** easily procure all we now relinquish. I am sure that I can be just as happy in a house that costs twenty pounds a-year as I can be in one at five times the rent. Cannot you be?"

"I ought to be happy anywhere with you. But the truth is, it wounds my pride to think of removing you to a lower condition. I would gladly place you on a throne, so to speak, if in my power."

"You cannot depress me below my true condition, nor elevate **me** above it," Mrs. Hartley said, half-smiling, half-serious. "There is One who sees the end from the beginning—One who governs all things with infinite wisdom—He will take care that I am ever in my right place. But I must be a co-worker with Providence, in freedom according to reason. The same is true, in regard to yourself. Let us then use the reason that has been given us, and act from its dictates, in perfect freedom from all selfishness or pride, or false views of our relations in life. If you seek my happiness, do it in this way, for in this way alone can you secure it."

Hartley could not withstand the force of truth from the lips of so eloquent a reasoner. Three weeks more elapsed. At the end of that time a snug little house in the district of Spring Garden held the young couple. Were they less happy? No! Hartley's salary was ample, and he felt that he was still independent, and that his wife had every comfort she desired. Their house **was no** less tastefully arranged than the one they had left. It was only smaller. But what of that? They had room enough and to spare.

"Is it not much better to be here," Anna said, as they sat together one evening in their little parlour, before a cheerful grate, "than for me to be **alone in a** larger house, and you away toiling, wearily, beyond your strength, to get the means of keeping up appearances? I am sure it is."

"Yes, Anna, it is better!" Hartley replied. "**We** were no happier before than we are now."

"Suppose we had rented the house in Walnut Street," Anna said, with an arch look.

"Hush!" and Hartley put his fingers on the lips of his wife, playfully. "Don't remind me of my weakness. If you had been a woman at all like Mrs. Riston, how quickly you might have ruined me!"

"And made you and myself both unhappy for life. I am not like her, James."

"No; thank Heaven! You are like nobody but your own dear self! You are a wise and prudent woman, and a loving wife."

"I can bear to hear my praises spoken by your lips," Anna returned, leaning her head back upon the breast of her husband, and looking up into his face with a fond happy smile.

"It comes from the heart—be sure of that."

"And reaches the heart ere the words are half-uttered," was the blushing reply.

CHAPTER XVI.

CONCLUSION.

THREE months more elapsed, when an event, looked for with hope and trembling anxiety, transpired. A new chord vibrated in Anna's heart, and the music was sweeter far in her spirit's ear, than any before heard. She was changed. Suddenly she felt that she was a new creature. Her breast was filled with deeper, purer, and tenderer emotions. She was a mother! A babe had been born to her! A sweet pledge of love lay nestling by her side, and drawing its life from her bosom. She was happy—how happy cannot be told. A mother only can *feel* how happy she was on first realizing the new emotions that thrill in a young mother's heart.

As health gradually returned to her exhausted frame, and friends gathered around her with warm congratulations, Anna felt that she was indeed beginning a new life. Every hour her soul seemed to enlarge, and her mind to be filled with higher and purer thoughts. Before the birth of her babe, she suffered much more than even her husband had supposed, both in body and mind. Her spirits were often so depressed, that it required her utmost effort to receive him with her accustomed cheerfulness at each period of his loved return. But living as she did in the ever active endeavour to bless others, she strove daily and hourly to rise above every infirmity. Now all was peace within—holy peace. There came a Sabbath rest of deep, interior joy, that was sweet, unutterably sweet. Body and spirit entered into this rest. No wind ruffled the still, bright waters of her life.

Hartley had loved his wife truly, deeply, tenderly. Every day he saw more and more in her to admire. There was an order, consistency, and harmony in her character **as** a wife, that won his admiration. In the few months they had passed since their marriage, she had filled her place to him perfectly. Without seeming to reflect how she should regulate her conduct towards **her** husband, in every act of her wedded **life** she had displayed true wisdom, united **with** unvarying love. All this caused his heart to unite itself more **and more** closely with hers. But now that she held **to him the** twofold relation of a wife and mother, his love **was** increased fourfold. He thought of her, and looked upon her, with increased tenderness.

"Mine by a double tie," he said, with a full realization of **his words,** when he first pressed his lips upon the brow **of his** child, and then, with a fervour unfelt before, **upon the lips of his wife.** "As **you have been a** good wife, you will be a good mother," he added, with emotion.

Hereafter we must know Mrs. Hartley in the twofold character of wife and mother, **for** they are inextricably blended. Thus far, scarcely a year has passed since the maiden became the wife. But little presents itself in the first year of a woman's married history of deep interest. Her life is more strongly marked internally than externally. She feels much, but the world sees little, and little can be brought forth to view. The little that we could present in the history of our gentle, true-hearted friend, with some strong contrasts, **has** been presented. Enough is apparent, we hope, to enable us to say to the young wife, "Go thou and do likewise." Enough to make all feel the loveliness of her example.

The change in her husband's external condition was good for them both. It tried their characters in the beginning, and, more than anything else that had occurred, made Hartley sensible of the real worth of a prudent and self-denying wife. Although months had elapsed since he was suddenly thrown down from a position so full of promise, into one comparatively discouraging to a man of an active, ambitious spirit, he still remained a clerk, with no prospect of rising above that condition. Had his wife seemed in the least degree to feel this change, it would have chafed him sorely. He would have been unhappy; but she was so cheerful and contented, and made everything so comfortable, and regulated her household expenses without appearing to think about doing so, according to her husband's reduced income, that he was rarely ever more than half-conscious while at home, that he was not in the receipt of over one-third of his former income.

If we were to lift for the reader, a moment or two, the veil that hides Mr. Riston and his wife from the public eye, a very different picture from this would be seen. But we care not to do so. The sayings and doings of Mrs. R. have already filled more than a fair proportion of our pages. Their moral needs no further expositions to give them force.

The Mother.

CHAPTER I.

INTRODUCTION.

SUMMER had passed away, and autumn had verged on towards winter. Instead of a brief, sultry twilight, there were long evenings and pleasant meetings of the family circle. Care looked more cheerful; there was a light on the wan cheek of Sickness; and Labour sung merrily as she turned her wheel.

His daily labours ended, James Hartley returned home on such an evening, his step light, his mind clear, and his spirits buoyant. Scarcely a year had passed since the wreck of his worldly prospects; but in that time the reacting strength of a manly character had lifted his bowed head, and fixed with confidence his steady eye. But this result would have taken place slowly and imperfectly under other circumstances and different influences from those with which he was surrounded. He owed much to the cheerful temper and hopeful spirit of his wife. So far from murmuring at the change in their prospects, or permitting her husband to murmur, every allusion to this change was accompanied by Mrs. Hartley with expressions of thankfulness that all the *real* blessings the world had to give were left them.

"We have more than enough for all our wants," she would say—"And besides, we have each other, and our dear little Marion. Do *you* think we have reason to complain? No—you cannot. Our cup is not empty—it is full to the brim."

As was ever the case, a smile of welcome greeted Hartley on entering his pleasant home. But it seemed to him, after the smile had died away, that there was a thoughtful expression upon Anna's brow. This grew distinct to his eye, as he observed her face more carefully.

"Is Marion asleep?" he asked, soon after he came in.

"Yes. She was tired, and went to sleep early. I tried to keep her awake until you came home, but she was so drowsy and fretful, that I thought it best to put her to bed."

"Dear little creature."

"She is a sweet child."

"A sweeter one cannot be found. As she grows older, how much delight we shall take in seeing her mind expand and become filled with images of all that is lovely and innocent. As the twig is bent, so is the tree inclined. Anna, all we have to do is to bend this twig aright. Heaven's rain and sunshine will do the rest."

"To bend it aright may not be so easy a task as you suppose, James."

"Perhaps not. And yet it seems to me that a wise course of government, carefully pursued, must produce the desired result."

"To determine wisely is not always in our power. Ah, James! It is that thing of determining *wisely* that gives me the greatest concern. I believe that I could faithfully carry out any system of government, were I only well satisfied of its being the true one. But so conscious am I, that, if in the system I adopt there be a vital error, the effect will be lastingly injurious to our child, that I hesitate and tremble at every step. The twig that shoots forth, unwarped by nature, pliant and graceful, may be trained to grow in almost any direction. But our child is born with an evil and perverse will—a will thoroughly depraved."

"That the human heart is by nature, not only deceitful, but desperately wicked, we know from God's own word."

"Alas! it *is* but too true, James. It needs not Revelation to tell us this. Already the moral deformity we have entailed upon our child is showing itself every day. How shall we correct it? How shall we change it into beauty? I think of this almost every hour, and sometimes it makes me feel sad. It is easy to say—'Just as the twig is bent the tree's inclined'—but it is not so easy a thing to bend the human twig as you will. There is great danger of creating one deformity in the effort to correct another; or of checking, in its flow, the healthy sap by undue pressure. And still further; our own states of mind, from various causes, are ever changing, and from these changes result obscurity, or a new direction of our thoughts. What seems of the first moment to-day, is not so considered to-morrow, because other ideas are more distinctly before our minds, and throw things of equal importance into obscurity. Our own uncorrected hereditary evils are also in our way, and hinder us from either seeing aright or doing aright."

"You are disposed to look at the gloomy side of the picture, Anna," repiled her husband, smiling. "Suppose you take a more encouraging view."

"Show me the bright side, James. I will look at it with pleasure."

"There is a bright side, Anna—everything has a sunny side; but I do not know that it is in my power to show you the sunny side of this picture. I will, however, present to your mind a truth that may suggest many others of an encouraging nature. Have we not the divine promise to those who train up a child in the way he should go, that when he is old he will not depart from it? Foolishness is indeed bound up in the **heart of** a child, but the Christian parent need not despond in the struggle to eradicate it. Can there **be a** higher or holier end than a mother's, when **she** proposes to herself the good of her **child?**"

"I believe not."

"Into that end will there most assuredly be an influx of wisdom to discover the true means. **Do not** despond, then. As your day is, so will your strength be."

Anna sighed heavily, but made no reply for some moments. She was too deeply conscious of the difficulty of applying the true means, to feel confidence in the practical bearing of the principles that her husband had declared, and which she so well knew were **true**.

"It is easy to theorize," **she at** length said. "It is pleasant to the mind to dwell upon true principles, and see how they apply in **real** life. But it is a different matter when we come to bring down these theories ourselves. There is in us so much that hinders—self-**love,** indolence, pride, and a thousand other things, come between our good purposes and their accomplishment."

"True. But on the side of good resolutions is One, **who is all**——"

"Right, my dear husband!—Right," exclaimed Anna, interrupting him. "**He** that is for us is more than all who are against us. If **I can** only fix my confidence, like an anchor of the soul, upon Him, all the rough places of peevish nature will be made even. Light will break in from a dark sky. I shall see clearly to walk in right paths."

"Ever let us both strive to fix our confidence upon God," responded Hartley in a low but earnest voice.

"If we do so, we shall not find our duty so hard to perform as at first sight it may appear to us. We must keep our minds elevated above all mere worldly and selfish ends, and seek only the highest good for our offspring."

"The highest good,—Yes, that must be our aim. But do we agree as to what *is* the highest good?"

"An important question, Anna. If we do not agree, our task will be a difficult one. What do you call the highest good?"

Anna mused for some time.

"The highest good—the highest good—" she murmured abstractedly. "Is it wealth?—Honour?—The love and praise of men?—The attainment of all earthly blessings?—No—no. These can only continue for a time. This life is a brief season at best—a mere point in our being—a state of preparation for our real and true existence. In seeking the highest good of our child we must seek first the kingdom of God, and his righteousness."

"If we do not, Anna, our seeking for the good of our child will be in vain. But, after determining *what* are the best interests of our child, the next great question is, *how* shall we secure them? Thousands have decided as we have, but alas! how few have been able to secure the right means. A religious education, I know to be the only true education. All others must fail. But what *is* a religious education? It is in the wrong determination of this question that so many fail."

"Can you determine it, James?"

"Is it not already determined for us in God's Word? Religion is heavenly order, and involves in it the true relation of the creature and the Creator. It is not the abstract, formal thing of mere outward show that so many make it; but a spirit of love ruling the heart, and of obedience to the divine will influencing every action of our lives. This we cannot give; but while we employ the means with her, we must ask of Him, who can alone bestow it, the sanctifying seal of the Holy Spirit."

"Most true; yet have you determined how we are to educate our child in such religious principles?"

"First of all we should, as I have already endeavoured to do, impress upon her mind the idea of a God, and that he loves her, watches over her, and protects her from harm. This is easily done. No idea is so readily conveyed to a child's mind as that of the existence of God as a good being. When I talk to Marion, young as she is, about God and the angels who live in heaven, she will look me steadily in the eyes, and listen with the most fixed attention. She cannot yet speak her thoughts, but I know that she more than half comprehends me, and that in her tender and still most impressible young mind, I am fixing ideas that can never be eradicated. As she grows older, and her mind expands, I shall not only teach her to regard the good of others, but instruct her in the right means of promoting it. The whole Law and the Prophets hang upon the precept, 'Thou shalt love the Lord thy God with all thy heart, and thy neighbour as thyself.' Here is the starting point in all religion. With this fundamental doctrine must all other doctrines square. To love God is to live according to his commandments; and to love our neighbour is to seek his good—his highest good. But it is God, as he was manifested in the flesh, the divine Redeemer, to whom I desire to lead our child. He who said, 'Suffer little children to come unto me, and forbid them not.' Oh! that I could do this as I desire."

CHAPTER II.

BEGINNING RIGHT.

This was the first serious conversation that had taken place between Mr. and Mrs. Hartley on the subject of the education of their child. As their thoughts became more and more steadily directed to the subject, they saw their duty clearer and clearer. At least such was the case with Mrs. Hartley, for hers was the task of making the first impression upon her child's mind— the first and most lasting impression. Upon the training of the mother depends, almost entirely, the future character and position of the child. No matter how wise and good the father may be, his influence will do but little if opposed to that of an injudicious mother. Take ten instances where men have risen from humble stations into eminence, and nine of these at least will be found the result of a mother's influence. Her love is a different one; it is more concentrated—and the more we love an object, the more accurate becomes our perception of the means of benefiting that object. The father is usually all absorbed in the pursuit of a business or profession by which to secure the temporal good of his family, and has little time, and too often less inclination, to devote himself to his children. When he retires into his family, his mind seeks rest from the over excitements of the day, and he is unprepared to give to his children judicious instruction, or to administer wise correction. He cannot adopt a system, and regularly carry it out, because he is with them only for a short time each day, and cannot know their characters thoroughly, nor the means that best re-act upon and keep their evils quiescent. Upon the mother devolves therefore, of necessity, the high and important duty of moulding the characters of her children—of impressing them for good or evil—of giving them true strength **for** their trials in after life.

Sensibly did Mrs. Hartley feel this. The path of duty lay clearly defined before her, and she shrunk not **from** walking therein. Love for her child, and an elevated sense of the duties of a Christian parent, were her prompters.

Her first efforts with her child, as reason began to dawn, were the best a mother can use. She sought to impress upon the mind of her little Marion one idea. Among the first words she taught her to say was the name of "Jesus;" and the child always uttered it with a quiet, earnest, thoughtful face, and pointed upwards. Soon the answer to "Who loves little Marion?" would be "Papa." "Who else?" "Mamma." "Who else?" "Jesus in heaven."

At every step she endeavoured to fix more deeply this impression. The lisped prayer on retiring to bed was never omitted.

The next effort she made was to counteract the selfish tendency of the child. She began with **teaching her** young mind to love God; the second step was to cause her to regard the good of others.

If her husband, from the very nature of his occupation, could not aid her much in the practical application of right means, he was ever ready to confer with **her,** and to aid her in discovering these means. **They** thought much, and conversed much together upon the subject.

The three great things to attain, as seeming of most importance to Mrs. Hartley in the education of her child, were to impress fervently and truly upon her mind a just idea of God; to **give** her an unselfish regard for her neighbour, and to insure perfect obedience. To do all this was a great work, **and** hard, almost impossible she often felt, to accomplish. But she strove unweariedly, yet not always wisely, after the attainment of her end; for she interfered with the freedom **of her** child—checked too often its innocent outbursts of exuberant feeling—saw too much, and let be seen **too fully by her child the** bonds with which she sought to hold her. The effect was consequently bad, for the rebound of her young spirits when away from her mother, was too strong. Instead of being happiest with her mother, she began to feel it a relief to escape from her presence.

Mrs. Hartley saw all this, and it grieved her deeply; but the cause she did not clearly perceive. Before, however, the evils of an over-rigid system had progressed too far, the birth of a second child divided her care and affection, and gave to Marion a real something that she could love understandingly.

CHAPTER III.

MEANS AND ENDS.

As month after month passed on, and Clarence, the latest born of Mrs. Hartley, began to exhibit some signs of his real disposition, the parents perceived, that it was very different from Marion's. The first born was quiet and easily controlled; but the boy was full of life, and showed very early a resolute will and passionate temper. Before he had completed a year, he had caused his mother many an anxious hour, and drawn from her eyes many a tear. From his sister he was disposed to take everything; and if his exacting spirit were **not** immediately gratified in its desires, he would scream violently, and sometimes throw himself passionately upon the floor. In the first year of her brother's life Marion had changed a good deal. Young as she was, her mother endeavoured to interest her in his favour —to lend him her play things when awake—and to rock his cradle when he was asleep, and do many little things for him within her ability to accomplish. To the exacting imperious temper of the child, Marion was much inclined to yield. To have permitted her to do so would have been the easiest course for Mrs. Hartley to pursue; but this she saw would be to injure both the children. It took some weeks after Mrs. Hartley began this important lesson before she seemed to make any impression. After that, the simple declaration, "This belongs to Marion," caused Clarence to yield at once. The achievement of so much gave the mother great encouragement. It was fruit to her labour, and the in-gathering even of so small a harvest was delightful.

As the boy added month after month and year after year to his age, his strengthening peculiarities of disposition became sources of constant anxiety to his mother.

"I am not fit to be a mother," she would sometimes say to her husband during these seasons of depression. "I lack patience and forbearance, and yet, I can see that Clarence has many very good qualities, and that these really overbalance the evil. His intellect is remarkably quick, and there is a manliness about him but rarely seen in children of his age."

"Persevere, Anna, persevere," were usually her husband's encouraging words. "You are doing well."

Time passed steadily on. Another and another babe saw the light, until five bright-eyed children filled their home with music and sunshine. When her care was lavished upon a single child, the mother had both mind and heart full. Now her duties were increased fivefold, but she did not feel them to be greater than at first. It seemed to her, when she had but one babe, that there was not room in her heart for another—but now she found that there was room for all. Each had its appropriate place.

Alike in some general features, these five children

were, in particulars, as unlike as possible. Marion, the eldest, was a sweet-tempered girl, ten years of age. Clarence had improved much under the careful training of his mother, though he was still rude, self-willed, and too little inclined to regard properly the rights and comforts of his brother and sisters. Henry, next younger than Clarence, was altogether opposite in character. Timid, bashful, and retiring, he had little confidence in himself, and was too much inclined to lean upon others. Fanny, a laughing little fairy thing, making the house musical with her happy voice, and Lilian, the babe, filled up the number of Mrs. Hartley's household treasures.

Nearly twelve years had passed since their marriage, and yet neither James Hartley nor his wife were very strongly marked by time. He had a more thoughtful, and she a more earnest expression of countenance. Their external condition had improved. He had again entered into business, though not with the flattering promises that before encouraged him to hope for a speedily attained fortune, but he was in a surer way to competency at least.

CHAPTER IV.

THE SECRET OF GOVERNING CHILDREN.

VERY soon after Mrs. Hartley assumed the responsible position of a mother, she became sensible that she had really more to do in the correction of what was wrong in herself, than in her children. To remain undisturbed at their disobedience, and unimpassioned when duty called her to administer correction, was next, it seemed to her, to impossible. A calm admonition she always saw did more good than an energetic one—and grief at her child's disobedience was ever more effective than anger. But anger was too ready to lift its distorted visage, and she mourned over this tendency with a real sorrow, because she saw that it exerted an unhappy influence, especially upon the self-willed, exciteable Clarence.

"I believe I have discovered a secret," she remarked to her husband, while they sat conversing one evening, about the time that Clarence attained his third year.

"What is that, dear?" he asked.

"The secret of governing my children easily."

"A great secret that. But are you sure you are right?"

"I think I am. It is to govern myself."

Mr. Hartley smiled.

"I believe it is the only true way," returned his wife.

"And so do I, Anna. But the government of ourselves is not so easy a matter."

"I am well aware of that. No one, it seems to me, can try harder than I do to control my feelings when Clarence does wrong. But I cannot do it once in ten times that I make the effort. When I do succeed, the task of correction is easy and effectual. A word, mildly but firmly uttered, or a look, is all that is required. The child seems at once subdued. I am sometimes astonished at so marked a result from what seems so small a cause."

"That you succeed once even in ten efforts, is certainly encouraging."

"It inspires me with the hope that I shall yet conquer myself, through the power sent me from above. The earnest love I feel for my children shall give me resolution to persevere.

"For their sakes persevere, dear Anna!" said her husband with emotion.

"I will," was her tearful answer—the drops of pure feeling were dimming her eyes.

How very few there are who think on this subject as did Mr. and Mrs. Hartley. Parents will indulge in all the evil tempers and dispositions of an unregenerate nature—will cherish envy and pride, hatred, malice, and all manner of selfishness, and yet wonder at their existence in their children. It is not to be wondered at that so few are successful in governing their children, when it is seen that they have not learned to govern themselves.

From this time both Mr. and Mrs. Hartley felt a new motive for striving after the correction in themselves of all perverted moral forms. The result was good. Mrs. Hartley found herself growing more patient and forbearing. She was able to stand, as it were, above her children, so as not to be affected by their bad tempers and dispositions with anything but an earnest and unimpassioned desire to correct them.

Having fairly set forth the principles of action which governed Mrs. Hartley in the management and education of her children, let us introduce her more fully to the reader, that she may be seen in the active effort to perform well a mother's part. The period already named, twelve years from the time of her marriage, will be the best for our purpose.

CHAPTER V.

A MOTHER'S INFLUENCE.

"There come the children from school," said Aunt Mary, a maiden sister of Anna's mother, as she was looking from the window. "Just see that Clarence! He'll have Henry in the gutter. I never saw such another boy. Why can't he come quietly along like other children? There!—now he must stop to throw stones at the pigs. That boy will give you the heart-ache yet, Anna."

Mrs. Hartley made no reply, but laid aside her work quietly, and left the room, to see that their dinner was ready. In a few minutes the street-door was thrown open, and the children came bounding in, full of life, and noisy as they could be.

"Where is your coat, Clarence?" she asked, in a pleasant tone, looking her oldest boy in the face.

"Oh, I forgot!" he replied cheerfully, and turning quickly, he ran down stairs, and lifting his coat from where, in his thoughtlessness, he had thrown it upon the floor, hung it up in its proper place, and then sprung up the stairs.

"Isn't dinner ready yet?" he said, with fretful impatience, his whole manner changing suddenly. "I'm hungry."

"It will be ready in a few minutes, Clarence."

"I want it now. I'm hungry."

"Did you ever hear of the man," said Mrs. Hartley, in a voice that showed no disturbance of mind, "who wanted the sun to rise an hour before its time?"

"No, mother. Tell me about it, will you?"

All impatience had vanished from the boy's face.

"There was a man who had to go a journey. The stage-coach was to call for him at sunrise. More than an hour before it was time for the sun to be up, the man was all ready to go, and for the whole of that hour he walked the floor impatiently, grumbling at the sun because he did not rise. 'I'm all ready, and I want to be going,' he said. 'It's time the sun was up, long ago.' Don't you think he was a very foolish man?"

Clarence laughed, and said he thought the man was very foolish indeed.

"Do you think he was more foolish than you were just now for grumbling because dinner wasn't ready?"

Clarence laughed again, and said he did not know. Just then, Hannah, the cook, brought in the waiter with the children's dinner upon it. Clarence sprang for a chair, and drew it hastily and noisily to the table.

"Try and see if you can't do that more orderly, my dear," his mother said, in a quiet voice, looking at him, as she spoke, with a steady eye.

The boy removed his chair, and then replaced it gently.

"That is much better, my son."

And thus she corrected his disorderly habits, quieted his impatient temper, and checked his rudeness, without showing any disturbance. This she had to do daily. At almost every meal she found it necessary to repress his rude impatience. It was line upon line, and precept upon precept; but she never tired, and rarely permitted herself to show that she was disturbed, no matter how deeply grieved she was at times over the wild and reckless spirit of her boy.

On the next day she was not very well. Her head ached badly all the morning. Hearing the children in the passage, when they came in from school at noon, she was rising from the bed where she had lain down, to attend to them, and give them their dinners, when Aunt Mary said:—

"Don't get up, Anna. I will see to the children."

It was rarely that Mrs. Hartley let any one do **for** them what she could do herself, for no one else could manage the impatient temper of Clarence. But so violent was the pain in her **head, that she let Aunt** Mary go, and sunk back upon the pillow **from which** she had arisen. A good deal of noise and confusion continued to reach her ears, **from** the **moment the** children came in. At length a loud cry and passionate words from Clarence caused her to rise up quickly and go to the dining-room. All was confusion there, and Aunt Mary out of humour, and scolding prodigiously. Clarence was standing up at the table, looking defiance at her, on account of some interference with his strong self-will. The moment the boy saw his mother, his countenance changed, and a look of confusion **took the** place of anger.

"Come to my room, Clarence," she said, in a low voice; there was sadness in its tones, that made him feel sorry that he had given vent so freely to his ill temper.

"What was the matter, my son?" Mrs. Hartley asked, as soon as they were alone, taking Clarence by the hand, and looking steadily at him.

"Aunt Mary wouldn't help me when I asked her."

"Why not?"

"She would help Henry first."

"No doubt she had a reason for it. Do you know her reason?"

"She said he was youngest." Clarence pouted out his lips, and spoke in a very disagreeable tone.

"Don't you think that was a very good reason?"

"I've as good a right to be helped first as he has."

"Let us see if that is so. You, and Marion, and Henry came in from school, all hungry and anxious for your dinners. Marion is oldest—she, one would suppose, from the fact that she is oldest, would be better able to feel for her brothers, and be willing to see their wants supplied before her own. You are older than Henry, and should feel for him in the same way. No doubt this was Aunt Mary's reason for helping Henry first. Had she helped Marion?"

"No, ma'am."

"Did Marion complain?"

"No, ma'am."

"No one complained but my unhappy Clarence. Do you know why you complained? I can tell you, as I have often told you before. It is because you indulge in very selfish feelings. All who do so make themselves miserable. If, instead of wanting Aunt Mary to help you first, you had, from a love of your little brother, been willing to see him first attended to, you would have enjoyed a real pleasure. If you had said, 'Aunt Mary, help Harry first,' I am sure Henry would have said instantly, 'No, Aunt Mary, help brother Clarence first.' How pleasant this would have been; how happy would all of us have felt at thus seeing two little brothers generously preferring **one** another!"

There was an unusual degree of tenderness, even sadness, in the voice of his mother, that affected Clarence. But he struggled with his feelings.—When, however, she resumed, and said—

"I have felt quite sick all the morning. My head has ached badly—so badly that I have had to lie down. I always give you your dinners when you come home, and try to make you comfortable. To-day I let Aunt Mary do it, because I felt so sick. But I am sorry that **I** did not get up, sick as I was, and do it myself—then **I** might have prevented this unhappy outbreak **of** my boy's unruly temper, that has made not only my head ache ten times as badly as it did, but my heart ache also—"

Clarence burst into tears, and throwing his arms around his mother's neck, wept bitterly.

"I will try and be good, dear mother!" he said. **"I** do try sometimes, but it seems that I can't."

"You must always try, my dear son. Now dry up your tears, and go out and get your dinner. Or, if you would rather I should go with you, I will do so."

"No, dear mother!" replied the boy, affectionately— "You are sick. You must not go. I will be good."

Clarence kissed his mother again, and then returned quietly to the dining-room.

"Naughty boy!" said Aunt Mary, as he entered, looking sternly at him.

A bitter retort came instantly to the tongue of Clarence, but he checked himself with a strong effort, and took his place at the table. Instead of soothing the quick-tempered boy, Aunt Mary chafed him by her words and manner during the whole meal, and it was only the image of his mother's tearful face, and the remembrance that she was sick, that restrained an outbreak of his passionate temper.

When Clarence left the table, he returned to his mother's room, and laid his head upon the pillow where hers was resting.

"I love you, mother," he said, affectionately—"You are good. But I hate Aunt Mary."

"O no, Clarence. You must not say that you hate Aunt Mary, for Aunt Mary is very kind to you. You mustn't hate anybody."

"She isn't kind to me, mother. She calls me a bad boy, and says everything to make me angry when I want to be good."

"Think, my son, if there is not some reason for Aunt Mary calling you a bad boy. You know yourself that you act very naughtily sometimes, and provoke Aunt Mary a great deal."

"But she said I was a naughty boy, when I went out just now; and I was sorry for what I had done, and wanted to be good."

"Aunt Mary didn't know that you were sorry, **I am** sure. **When** she called you 'naughty boy,' what did you say?"

"I was going to say, 'you're a fool!' but I didn't. I tried hard not to let my tongue say the bad words, though it wanted."

"Why did you try not to say them?"

"Because it would have been wrong, and would **have** made you feel sorry; and I love you." Again the repentant boy kissed her. His eyes were full of **tears**, and so were the eyes of his mother.

While talking over this incident with her husband, Mrs. Hartley said—

"Were not all these impressions so light, I should feel encouraged. The boy has warm and tender feelings, but I fear that his passionate temper and selfishness will, like evil weeds, completely check their growth."

"The case is bad enough, Anna, but not so bad, I hope, as you fear. These good affections are never active in vain. They leave upon the mind an indelible impression. In after years the remembrance of them will revive the states they produced, and give strength to good desires and intentions. Amid all his irregularities and wanderings from good, **in** after life, the thoughts of his mother will restore the feelings he had to-day, and draw him back from evil with cords of love that cannot be broken. The good now implanted will remain, and, like ten just men, save the city. **In** most instances where men abandon themselves finally to evil courses, it will be found that the impressions made in childhood were not of the right kind—that the mother's influence was not what it should have been. For myself, I am sure that a different mother would have made me a different man. When a boy, I was too much like Clarence; but the tenderness with which my mother always treated me, and the unimpassioned but earnest manner in which she reproved and corrected my faults, subdued my unruly temper. When I became restless or impatient, she always had a book to read to me, or a story to tell, or had some device to save me from myself. My father was neither harsh nor indulgent towards me; I cherish his memory with respect and love. But I have different feelings when I think of my mother. I often feel even now as if she were near me—as if her cheek were laid to mine. My father would *place his hand upon my head*, caressingly, but my mother would *lay her cheek against mine*. I did not expect my father to do more—I do not know that I should have loved him had he done more; for him it was a natural expression of affection. But no act is too tender for a mother. Her kiss upon my cheek, her warm embrace, are all felt now; and the older I grow the more holy seem the influences that surrounded me in childhood. To-day I cut from a newspaper some verses that pleased and affected me. I have brought them home. Let me read them to you.

ANNA LEE,

"'I DREAMED OF MY MOTHER.'"*

"I dreamed of my mother, and sweet to my soul
Was the brief-given spell of that vision's control;
I thought she stood by me, all cheerful and mild,
As when to her bosom I clung as a child.

Her features were bright with the smiles that she wore,
When heeding my idle-tongued prattle of yore;
And her voice had that kindly and silvery strain
That from childhood had dwelt in the depths of my brain.

She spoke of the days of her girlhood and youth—
Of life and its cares, and of hope and its truth;
And she seemed as an angel winged from above,
To bring me a message of duty and love.

She told of her thoughts at the old village school—
Of her walks with her playmates when loosed from its rule—
Of her rambles for berries; and when they were o'er
Of the mirth-making groups at the white cottage door.

She painted the garden, so sweet to the view,
Where the wren made its nest, and the pet flowers grew—
Of the trees that she loved for their scent and their shade,
Where the robin, and wild-bee, and humming-bird played.

And she spoke of the greenwood which bordered the farm
Where her glad moments glided unmixed with alarm;—
Of the well by the wicket whose waters were free,
And the lake with its white margin traversed in glee.

And she pondered, delighted, the joys to retrace
Of the family scenes of that ruralized place—
Of its parties and bridals, its loves and its spells—
Its heart-clinging ties and its saddened farewells.

She pictured the meeting-house, where, with the throng,
She heard the good pastor and sang the sweet song—

* By Thomas G. Spear.

Of the call from the pulpit—the feast at the shrine,
And the hallowed communings with feelings divine.

'And listen, my son,' she did smilingly say,
'If 'tis pleasant to sing, it is sweeter to pray—
If the future is bright in the day of thy prime,
That brightness may grow with the fading of time.

* * * * *

Look up to thy Maker, my son, and rejoice!'
Was the last gentle whisper that came from her voice,
While its soft, soothing tones on my dreaming ear fell,
As she glided away with a smiling farewell.

There are dreams of the heavens, and dreams of the earth,
And dreams of disease that to phantoms give birth,
But the hearer of angels, awake or asleep,
Has a vision of love to remember and keep.

I awoke from the spell of that vision of night,
And inly communed with a quiet delight,
And the past, and the present, and future surveyed,
In the darkness presented by fancy, arrayed.

I thought of the scenes when that mother was nigh,
In a soft sunny land, and beneath a mild sky,
When at matins we walked to the health-giving spring,
With the dew on the grass and the birds on the wing—

Of the draughts at the fount as the white sun arose,
And the views from the bluffs where the broad river flows—
Of the sound from the shore of the fisherman's train,
And the sight of the ship as it sailed to the main—

Of the wild flowers plucked from the glen and the field,
And the beauties the meadows and gardens revealed—
Of all that she paused to explain or explore,
Till I learned, in my wonder, to think and adore.

And of joys that attended the fireside scene,
When woodlands and meadows no longer were green—
Of the sports and the tales and the holiday glee,
That ever were rife at the fond mother's knee—

Of the duties of home, and the studies of school,
With the many delights that divided their rule,
Till the sunshine of boyhood had ended, and brought
The cares and the shadows of manhood and thought.

And I sighed for the scenes that had faded away—
For the forms that had fallen from age to decay—
For the friends who had vanished, while looking before,
To paths that their feet were forbid to explore.

And glancing beyond, through the vista of time,
With a soul full of hope, and with life in its prime.
Though flowers by memory cherished had died,
Life's garden was still with some blossoms supplied.

And oft as that dream to my spirit comes back,
A newness of thought re-illumines my track."—

* * * * *

"Pure and tender. The mother who called forth that heart-warm tribute was, doubtless, a good mother," said Anna.

"You remember Cowper's lines, written on receiving his mother's picture?" remarked her husband, after musing for a short time.

"Oh, yes. Very well. They have often affected me to tears,—

'O that those lips had language! Life has passed
With me but roughly since I heard thee last.
Those lips are thine—thy own sweet smile I see,
The same that oft in childhood solaced me;
Voice only fails, else how distinct they say—
Grieve not, my child, chase all thy fears away.'"

"To him, how great was the loss he sustained in the death of his mother. Had she lived, the deep melan-

THE MOTHER.

choly that seized him in after life might never have occurred. With what simple eloquence he describes his loss." And Mr. Hartley repeated a passage of the poem.

> "My mother! when I learned that thou wast dead,
> Say, wast thou conscious of the tears I shed?
> Hovered thy spirit o'er thy sorrowing son,
> Wretched, e'en then, life's journey just begun?
> Perhaps thou gav'st me, though unfelt, a kiss.
> Perhaps a tear, if souls can weep in bliss,—
> Ah, that maternal smile! it answers—Yes.
> I heard the bell toll on thy burial day,
> I saw the hearse that bore thee slow away,
> And turning from my nursery window, drew
> A long, long sigh, and wept a last adieu!
> But was it such?—It was.—Where thou art gone
> Adieus and farewells are a sound unknown.
> May I but meet thee on that peaceful shore,
> Thy parting word shall pass my lips no more!
> Thy maidens grieved themselves at my concern,
> Oft gave me promise of thy quick return.
> What ardently I wished, I long believed,
> And disappointed still, was still deceived.
> By expectation every day beguiled,
> Dupe of *to-morrow* even from a child.
> Thus many a sad to-morrow came and went,
> 'Till, all my stock of infant sorrow spent,
> I learned at last submission to my lot,
> But, though I less deplored thee, ne'er forgot."

Mrs. Hartley leaned her head upon her husband's shoulder, unable to restrain the tears that were springing to her eyes.

"If Heaven only spares me to my children, it is all I ask," she murmured. "I will be patient with and forbearing towards them. I will discharge my duties with unwearied diligence. Who can fill a mother's place? Alas! no one. If any voice had been as full of love for him when a child, if any hand had ministered to him as tenderly, this touching remembrance of his mother would never have been recorded by Cowper:—

> ' Thy nightly visits to my chamber made,
> That thou might'st find me safe and warmly laid;
> Thy morning bounties ere I left my home,
> The biscuit or confectionary plum;
> The fragrant waters on my cheeks bestowed
> By thy own hand, 'till fresh they shone and glowed,
> All this, and more endearing still than all,
> Thy constant flow of love, that knew no fall,
> Ne'er roughened by those cataracts and breaks
> That humour interposed too often makes.
>
> *   *   *   *   *
>
> Could Time, his flight reversed, restore the hours
> When, playing with thy vesture's tissued flowers,
> The violet, the pink, and jessamine,
> I pricked them into paper with a pin,
> (And thou wast happier than myself the while,
> Wouldst softly speak, and stroke my head and smile)
> Could those few pleasant days again appear.
> Might one wish bring them, would I wish them here?
> I would not trust my heart—the dear delight
> Seems so to be desired, perhaps I might—
> But no—what here we call our life is such,
> So little to be loved, and thou so much,
> That I should ill requite thee to constrain
> Thy unbound spirit into bonds again.' "

"Ah, who could be unkind to a motherless one?"

"The lot of an orphan child is not always as sad a one as must have been that of young Cowper," said Mr. Hartley, "for it is but rarely that a child possesses the delicate or rather morbid sensibility that characterised him."

"I could not bear to think that any child of mine would remember me with less tenderness," replied Mrs. Hartley.

"Even though it embitter his whole life."

"No—no. It was the mother's selfishness, not the mother's love that spoke," she instantly returned.

"To recur to what we were first talking about," said Mr. Hartley, after a pause. "There cannot be a doubt that the whole life of the child is affected by the mother's character, and the influences she has brought to bear upon him. I could point to many instances that have come under my observation to illustrate this. The father of one of my schoolmates was a man of highly cultivated mind and polished manners; his mother was the reverse. The son is like the mother. As a man he did not rise in society at all, and is now the keeper of a billiard saloon. In another instance, the father was a low-minded man, and inclined to dissipation. Nearly the whole burden of the support of the family fell upon the mother; but her children always came to school neat and clean. Their behaviour was good, and they studied with diligence. Only one of four sons turned out badly. Three of them are now merchants in good business; and the mother's declining years are blessed by their kindest attentions. You see then, Anna, how much you have to encourage you."

"If there were nothing to encourage me, love and duty would make me persevere."

"But there is much. 'Cast thy bread upon the waters, and it shall be found after many days.'"

CHAPTER VI.

CORRECTING A FAULT.

"There are two faults in Clarence and Henry," said Mrs. Hartley one day to her husband, "that I am at a loss how to correct. They are bad faults, and will affect their characters through life, if not judiciously corrected now. Clarence looks with an envious eye upon everything that Henry has, and manages, sooner or later, to get possession of it by his brother's consent. Henry soon tires of what he has, and is easily induced to part with it to Clarence for some trifling consideration. It is not long, however, before he wants it back again, and then trouble ensues. Sometimes I think I will make a law that neither Clarence nor his brother shall part with anything that has been given to him. But I am afraid of the effect of this. It will foster a selfish spirit. It will allow of no generous self-sacrifice for the good of others."

"I think with you, that the effect would not be good. Still, it is very important that a certain feeling of property in what each one has should be preserved. As far as this can be accomplished, without strengthening the selfish tendency of our nature, it should be done. It causes each one not only to protect his own rights, but to regard the rights of his neighbours."

"I see all that very clearly. The happy medium is what I desire to attain. As things are now, the disposition which Clarence has to appropriate everything to himself is fostered, and Henry is losing that just regard to his own rights that he ought to have. Now, what ought I to do? Can you devise a plan?"

"Not so well as you can. But let me see. Suppose you try this mode for a while. Make a law, that if Henry give Clarence any of his playthings, the right to possess them shall be as perfect as if you or I had presented them to Clarence as his own. The practical working of this will, in a short time, make Henry reflect a little before he relinquishes his property to his brother."

"That will do, I think," said Mrs. Hartley. "There will be no harm in trying it at any rate."

On the next day she gave Clarence a new book, and Henry a humming-top.

"Now let me tell you something," she said. "This book belongs to you, Clarence, and this top to you, Henry. I hope they will please you very much, and that you will take good care of them. You can lend them to each other, if you choose; but I would rather you would not give them to each other. Should either of you do so, the one who gives his book or his top away cannot reclaim it. Do you understand, Henry?"

"O yes, ma'am, I understand; I'm not going to give anybody my top, I know."

"Very well, my son. You can do so if you wish; but remember, after you have once given it away you cannot get it back again."

"Why can't I, mother?" asked the little boy.

"Because, after you have given anything away, it is no longer yours."

"I'm not going to give it away," he said, in a positive voice, as he ran off to spin his top in the playroom.

For about an hour Clarence was very much interested in his book, while Henry continued to spin his top with undiminished pleasure. After this time the interest of Clarence began to flag, and the sound of Henry's humming-top came more and more distinctly to his ears from the adjoining room. At last he closed the book and sought his brother.

"Let me spin it once, won't you, Henry?" he said.

"Yes, I will," returned the generous-minded boy, and instantly handed the top and cord to Clarence, who wound it up, and sent it humming and skipping about the floor at a fine rate.

Henry reached out his hand for the cord, but his brother held it back, saying,

"Just let me spin it once more."

"Well, you may once more," was replied.

But it was "once more," and "once more," until Henry's tears restored to him his toy.

"You are a selfish fellow," said Clarence, as he flung the top and cord at his brother's feet.

Clarence did not resume his book, but stood looking at Henry's top, as he spun it, with a covetous expression on his face.

"If you'll let me spin your top, you may read my book," he at length said.

"I will," quickly returned Henry.

The top and book were exchanged, and, for a time, both were well pleased. But the book was rather beyond the grasp of Henry's mind. He soon tired of it.

"You may have your book now, Clarence. I've done reading it. Give me my top."

"I've not done with it yet. I let you read my book until you were tired, and now you must let me spin your top until I am tired."

Henry rarely contended with his brother: he did not like contention. Knowing how resolute Clarence was in doing anything that suited his humour, he said no more, but went and sat down quietly upon a little chair, and looked on wishfully while Clarence spun his top.

It was half an hour before Henry again got possession of his top, but the zest with which he had at first played with it was gone. After spinning it for a few times he said—

"Here, Clarence, you may have it. I don't **want** it."

"May I have it altogether?" eagerly asked Clarence.

"Yes, you may!"

"You'll want it back?"

"No, I won't. You may keep it **for** ever."

Clarence took possession of the **top with** right good will, and went on spinning **it to his** heart's content. After dinner Henry wanted it back again, and when his brother refused **to give it up,** went crying to his mother. Mrs. Hartley called up Clarence, and asked him why he did not give Henry his top.

"It isn't his top, mother; it is mine," said Clarence.

"Yours! How came it yours?"

"Henry gave it to me."

"Did you give it to him, Henry?"

"Yes, ma'am, this morning; but it's my top, and **I** want it."

"No, it is not your top any longer, if you have given it to Clarence. It is his, and he must keep it. Have you forgotten what I told you when I gave it to you? If you give away your things, they are no longer yours, and you cannot expect to get them back again. I hope, my son, that hereafter you will be more careful what you do."

Henry cried bitterly, but his mother would not compel Clarence, upon whom Henry's tears had no effect, to restore the toy. The poor little fellow's heart **was** almost broken at this hard lesson in the school of human life.

In about a week Mrs. Hartley tried it over again. Gifts were made to the children, and soon Clarence went to work to get possession of what his brother had. But Henry had not forgotten the top, and was, therefore, not so generous as before. He withstood every effort for the first day. On the second, however, he yielded. On the following day he reclaimed his toys; but his mother interposed again, and maintained Clarence's right to what Henry had given him.

The poor child seemed unable to comprehend the justice of this decision, and grieved so much about it that Mrs. Hartley felt unhappy. But ultimate good, she was sure, would be the result, painful as it might be to correct her child's fault.

On the next occasion, Clarence found it much harder to prevail upon Henry to give him his playthings than before. The same result following, the little fellow's eyes began to be opened. He would consider the consequences, and think when Clarence wanted him to give him anything; and the recollection of the permanent losses he had already sustained, at length gave him the resolution to persevere in refusing to yield up his right to anything that had been given to him. He would lend whatever he had, cheerfully; but when asked to give, he generally said—

"No.—If I give it to you, I can't get it back again."

The parents did not like to check the generous spirit of their child, but they felt that it was necessary both for his good and the good of his brother, that he should be taught to set a higher value upon what was his own. If he were not led **to do** this while young, it might prevent his usefulness when a man, by leaving him the prey of every one. Besides, the want of a due regard to his own property in anything was not right.

Another fault in Henry they felt bound to visit with a rigid system of correction. He was naturally **an** obedient child, while his brother was the reverse. He was also very yielding, and could easily be persuaded by Clarence to join in acts which were forbidden by their parents. When called to account, his usual excuse was, that he had been asked by Clarence, or had gone with him. He did not appear to think that he was to blame for anything if he **acted** upon his elder brother's suggestions. The only way to correct this, was to let each be punished for offences mutually committed, even though Henry **was** far less to blame than Clarence. It was only by doing so, the parents felt, that Henry could be made to see that he must be held responsible for his own acts. This course soon effected all they desired. Clarence was usually alone in all flagrant violations of parental authority.

CHAPTER VII.

STRONG CONTRAST.

Nearer than Mrs. Hartley had supposed, lived for many years an old but now almost forgotten friend—Florence Armitage; or rather, Mrs. Archer.

The house in which she lives is a small comfortless one, in an obscure street not far from the residence of Mr. and Mrs. Hartley. Her father has become poor, and her husband, whose habits are more irregular than when a single man, receives a small salary as clerk, more than half of which he spends in self-indulgence; the other half is eked out to his wife, who, on this pittance, is compelled to provide for five children. She has had six, but one is dead.

It was a clear bright evening without, but there was nothing cheerful in the dwelling of William Archer. The supper table was on the floor, and on it burned a poor light. The mother sat near the table, with an infant on her lap, mending a pair of dark stockings with coarse yarn of a lighter colour. A little girl three years of age was swinging on her chair, and a boy two years older was drumming on the floor with two large sticks, making a deafening noise.. This noise Mrs. Archer bore as long as she could, when her patience becoming exhausted, she cried out in a loud fretful voice—

"You, Bill; stop that noise!"

The boy paused for a single moment, and then resumed his amusement.

"Did you hear me, Bill? you heedless wretch!" exclaimed the mother, after she had borne the sound for some time longer.

There was silence for about a minute, and the noise began again.

"If you don't stop that, Bill, I'll box your ears soundly!" screamed the impatient mother.

The boy stopped for the space of nearly two minutes this time; then he went on again with his drumming.

"Do you want me to send you to bed without any supper?"

"No, I don't," replied the child.

"Then hush that noise, or I shall certainly send you to bed. You set me almost crazy."

Bill, as his mother called him, laid himself back upon the floor, and commenced kicking up his heels. After having amused himself in this way for some time, his drum-sticks were again resorted to, and the room was once more filled with the distracting din he made. Mrs. Archer bore it as long as she could, and then she boxed the child's ears soundly.

After the cries this operation extorted had died away, all was quiet enough for a quarter of an hour, when Mr. Archer came in to tea.

Twelve years had changed him sadly. His brow was

gloomy, his eyes sunken, and his lips closely drawn together, giving his countenance an expression of sternness. He looked at least twenty years older. He did not even cast his eyes upon his wife as he entered, but drew a chair to the table, and taking a newspaper from his pocket, began reading it.

"Bill, go and tell Jane to bring up tea," said Mrs. Archer.

The child went out into the passage, and cried down to the cook in a tone of authority—

"Bring up tea, will you?"

No notice of this was taken by the parents. Jane came up with the tea, looking as sulky as possible.

"Here, take the baby," said Mrs. Archer, handing Jane the child in a most ungracious manner. Jane took the child quite as ungraciously as it was tendered, and managed to keep it crying most of the time they were at supper.

"Where is John?" asked Mr. Archer, looking up at his wife, when about half through with his silent meal.

"Dear knows, for I don't. He came in from school, but was off at once, as usual. He is going to ruin as fast as ever a boy was."

"Why do you let him run the streets in this way?"

"He's got beyond me. I don't pretend to try to manage him. I might just as well tell him to go as stay; it would be all the same to him. It's high time you had taken him in hand, I can tell you. Florence is at her grandmother's, and I intended sending John for her an hour ago; but he hasn't shown himself."

Mr. Archer did not reply; he felt worried and angry. While they were yet at the table, John, a lad of some eleven years old, came in, and threw his hat down in the corner.

"Go and hang your hat up, sir," said his father. "Is that the place for it?"

John did as he was ordered.

"Now, where have you been, sir?" was the father's angry interrogation.

"I've been playing."

"What business have you to go off without **asking** your mother? I've a great mind to take off your jacket for you, sir. If ever I hear of this again, **I'll** give you such a lacing as you've never **had in your** life. Don't sit down to the table there! **Go, put on** your hat again, and be off for your sister."

"Where is she?"

"Where is she?" mimicking the tones and manner of the boy. "At your grandmother's," said Mr. Archer. "Go along after her, and be quick; she ought to have been at home more than an hour ago."

John went out slowly and sulkily.

"If that boy goes to ruin, you will have no one to blame but yourself," said Mr. Archer, ill-naturedly.

"I don't know how you are going to make that out,"

returned his wife in a voice quite as amiable as that in which he had spoken.

"You have no government over him."

"I have quite as much as yourself," retorted Mrs. Archer.

"Humph! You don't think so, do you?"—he spoke in a sneering tone.

"I think just what I say. If you paid the least attention to your children, they would grow up very differently. Instead of staying at home, and trying to make something of them, you are off every night, nobody knows where; but after no good, of course."

"Hold your tongue, will you!" Mr. Archer gave his wife an angry scowl as he said this.

The wife felt little inclination to contend further. There was a brutality in her husband's tone and manner that stunned her. She said nothing more.

While the father and mother were engaged in a war of words, the little boy before mentioned was amusing himself by spinning his spoon round in his plate, which made a most annoying clatter, and served to add to the irritation felt by both Mr. and Mrs. Archer, although the cause was not noticed until their contention was over.

The mother laid her hand upon the boy's head, and said, "Don't make that noise, Bill; you distract me."

But the moment the pressure of the hand was removed, like a re-acting spring the movement went on again; the noise, if anything, louder than ever. A vigorous box on the ear signified that poor Mrs. Archer's patience was exhausted. Almost simultaneously with the loud scream of the child came the loud bang of the **door.** **Her** husband had precipitately left the **house.**

Jane, the cook, who was nursing the babe, waited patiently **for some** time after Archer had left, to be called upon from the kitchen. But minute after minute passed, and no summons came. It was nearly a quarter of an hour before she ascended to the dining-room. She found Mrs. Archer in a state of entire abstraction, with her head resting on her hand. The little boy was fast asleep in his chair.

The mother roused up on the entrance of the cook, and said—

"Here, Jane, give me the baby, and **take** this child up and put him to bed before you clear off the table." The fair young face and glowing cheeks of the little boy, as Jane lifted him up, met the mother's eye. She sighed deeply, and again fell into her former dreamy state.

In a little while John and Florence came in. Florence was a sweet-faced child, just nine years old. Her disposition was mild, and she was very thoughtful, rendering her mother much service in her attentions to the younger children. Her first act was to go up to her mother and kiss her, and then kiss the babe that lay upon her lap.

"Have you had a pleasant time, dear?" asked Mrs. Archer.

"O yes, mother. I have had a nice time. Grandma baked us a whole basket full of cakes, which I have brought home; and she let me help her. I cut them all out. Where is Willy and Mary?" she added, looking around. "They must have some cakes. Oh, dear! Here's sis' fast asleep on the floor. Shall I wake her up, mother, and give her a cake?"

"No, dear, I wouldn't wake her now. The cakes will taste just as good to her in the morning."

"Where is Willy?"

"He's in bed. Jane took him up stairs."

"Shall I hold the baby, while you undress Mary?" asked Florence, as she took off her bonnet and shawl.

"Yes, you may."

"Dear little baby!" murmured Florence, as she took the child from her mother's arms, and sat down with it upon a low stool.

"I want some supper," said John, pouting out his lips, and looking as ugly and ill-natured as possible.

"There's some bread and butter for you. Sit down and eat that, and then take yourself off to bed," replied his mother.

"I want some tea."

"You'll not get any."

"I'll go and ask Jane to give me some."

"Take care, sir, or you'll be sent off without a mouthful."

With as bad a grace as possible, John sat down upon the corner of a chair, and commenced eating. The moment his mother left the room with Mary in her arms, his hand was in the sugar-bowl, a portion of the contents of which were freely laid upon his bread and butter.

"If I don't get tea, I'll have sugar," he said.

He was in the act of helping himself from the sugar-bowl for the third time, when his mother came in. The consequence was, that he got his ears soundly boxed, and was sent off to bed.

Florence continued to nurse the babe, or rock it in the cradle, for an hour, when she became too sleepy to hold up her head. Kissing her mother affectionately, the child said good night, and went off alone to her room, where she undressed herself and retired for the night. But no prayer was said; her mother had never taught her this best of infantile lessons.

Mrs. Archer sat up sewing until nearly eleven o'clock, and then sought her pillow. As usual, her husband had not yet returned. It was past midnight when he came home.

Too many of the evenings that were passed in the family of Mr. and Mrs. Archer were similar to the one we have described.

CHAPTER VIII.

MORE CONTRASTS.

Five more years of patience, forbearance, and anxious solicitude passed, and Mrs. Hartley began to see many good results of her labour, especially when she contrasted the habits and manners of her own children with the habits and manners of the children of some of her friends.

One of these friends, a Mrs. Fielding, had four children of naturally very good dispositions. They were affectionate to one another, and seemed to have more than usual love of home about them. The mother's fireside circle might have been an earthly paradise, if she had been at all disposed to consult her children's good, instead of her own pleasure. But this she was not disposed to do. She was vain, and fond of company. When she had provided a good nurse for her children, she thought that her duty was done. It never occurred to her that her children needed a companion, such as only she could be to them, as much as they needed a nurse to provide for their bodily comfort.

This woman came in to see Mrs. Hartley one day, and found her sitting at the piano.

"What does all this mean?" asked Mrs. Fielding, in a gay tone. "You playing the piano! I thought you had enough else to do."

"I'm only practising for the children."

"What good will your practising do the children, I wonder?"

"A good deal, I hope. We have frequently a little family party among ourselves, when the children dance, and I play for them."

"And you practise for this purpose during the day! I wonder how you find time—you who are such a slave to your family!"

"If everything is done according to a regular system, we can easily find time for almost anything."

"I don't know. You beat me out. I do scarcely anything in my family, it seems; and yet I am always hurried to death when I do that little, so that it isn't more than half done. As to practising on the piano, that is out of the question."

Mrs. Hartley faintly sighed.

"You have four sweet children," she said, after a pause; "I never saw better dispositions, naturally, in my life. You might do anything with them you pleased."

"What you say, a mother's partiality aside, is true," replied Mrs. Fielding, with a brightening face. "They are all good children. I only wish I was a better mother—that I was like you, Mrs. Hartley. I fear I am too fond of society; but I can't help it."

"Oh, don't say that, Mrs. Fielding. Love for our children should be strong enough to make us correct anything in ourselves that stands in the way of their good. A mother's duties ought to take precedence of everything else."

"I don't think a mother ought to be a slave to her children."

"Willing servitude is not slavery. How can you use such a word in connection with a mother? Her devotion should be from a love that never wearies—never grows cold."

"I don't know how that may be; mine wearies often enough."

"I feel discouraged sometimes," replied Mrs. Hartley. "But my love never abates. It grows stronger with every new difficulty that is presented."

"You are one in a thousand, then; that is all I can say. I know a good many mothers, and I know that they all complain bitterly about the trouble they have with their children."

"They would have less trouble, if they loved them more."

"How can you make that appear?"

"Love ever strives to benefit its object. A true love for children prompts the mother to seek with the most self-sacrificing assiduity for the means of doing her offspring good."

"Oh, dear! I'm sadly afraid I am not a true mother then. It's no use to disguise it—I cannot give up every comfort for my children; and I don't think we are required to do it."

"True love, Mrs. Fielding, sacrifices nothing when it is in pursuit of its object; for it desires nothing so ardently as the attainment **of that** object. I am not aware that I give up every comfort. I sometimes, **it is** true, deny myself a gratification, because, in seeking **it, I** must neglect my children, or interfere with their pleasures; but I have never done this that I have not been more than repaid for all I thought I had lost."

"Well, that is **a** comfort. I only wish I could say as much."

"You would soon be able to say so, if you were to make sacrifices for your children from love to them."

"I think I do love them."

"I am sure of that, Mrs. Fielding. But, to **speak** plainly, as one friend may venture to speak to **another,** perhaps you love yourself more."

"Perhaps I do. But how is that to be determined?"

"Very easily. **We love** those most who occupy most of our thoughts, and for whose comfort and happiness we are most careful, whether it be ourselves or our children."

Mrs. Fielding did not reply. Mentally she applied **the** rule, and was forced to acknowledge that she loved herself more than she did her children.

The oldest boy of Mrs. Fielding was about the same age as Clarence. Having completed all their preparatory studies, the two boys were sent the same year to college. At the age of sixteen, they left their homes for the first time, to be absent, except at short intervals, for three years. James Fielding left home with reluctance.

"I don't want to go, mother," he said the day before he was to start.

"Why not, James?" she asked.

"I would rather go to school here. I can learn just as much."

"Yes; but think of the honour, my son, of passing through college. It isn't every boy that has this privilege. It will make a man of you. I hope you will do credit to yourself and your parents. You must strive for the first honours. Your father took them before you."

Very different was the parting counsel of Mrs. Hartley to her son. The question whether it would be best in the end to send their son to college, was long and anxiously debated between the father and mother. Many reasons, for and against, were presented, and these were scanned minutely. The strongest objection felt by them was the fact that, from the congregating together of a large number of young men at college, among whom would be many with loose principles and bad habits, there would be danger of moral contamination. For a time they inclined to the belief that it would be better not to send their son from home; but their anxiety to secure for him the very best education the country afforded, at last determined them.

Long and earnestly did Mrs. Hartley commune with her boy on the evening before his departure.

"Never forget, my son," she said, "the end for which you should strive after knowledge. It is, that you may be better able, by your efforts as a man, to benefit society. A learned man can always perform higher uses than an ignorant man. And remember, that one so young and so little acquainted with the world as yourself, will be subjected to many severe temptations. But resist evil with a determined spirit. Beware of the first deviation from right. Suffer not the smallest stain to come upon your garments. Let your mother receive you back as pure as when you went forth, my son.

"You will discover, soon after you enter college, a spirit of insubordination—a disposition in many of the students to violate the laws of the institution; but do not join with them. It is just as wrong for a student to violate the laws of a college, as it is for a citizen to violate the laws of his country. They are wholesome regulations, made for the good of the whole; and he who weakens their force does a wrong to the whole. Guard yourself here, my son, for here you will be tempted. But stand firm. If you break, wilfully, a college law, your honour is stained, and no subsequent obedience can efface it. Guard your honour, my dear boy! It is a precious and holy thing.

"I will write to you often, and you must write often

MOTHER AND SON.

Page 236.

to me. Talk to me, in your letters, as freely as you would talk if we were face to face. Consider me your best friend; and he who would weaken my influence over you, as your worst enemy. You cannot tell, my son, how anxious I feel about you. I know, far better than you can know, how intimately danger will surround you. But, if you will make God's holy law, as written in his Ten Commandments, the guide of your life, you will be safe. Christian, in his journey to the land of Canaan, had not a path to travel in more beset with evil than will be yours, but you will be safe from all harm, if, like him, you steadily resist and fight against everything that would turn you from the straight and narrow way of truth and integrity. You go with your mother's blessing upon your head, and your mother's prayers following you."

The earnestness with which his mother spoke, affected the heart of Clarence. He did not reply, but he made a firm resolution to do nothing that would give her a moment's pain. He loved her tenderly; for she had ever been to him the best of mothers, and this love was his prompter.

"I will never pain the heart of so good a mother," he said, as he laid his head upon his pillow that night. How different might have been his feelings, if he had been brought up under different maternal influences.

CHAPTER IX.

FRUIT.

About the same time that Clarence Hartley was sent to college, the eldest son of Mr. Archer was sent to sea as the last hope of reclaiming him. He had been suffered to run into all kinds of bad company until he was so degraded that his mother lost all control over him. And yet this boy had naturally a more obedient temper than Clarence, and could have been managed far more easily. It is true that the two mothers were placed under different circumstances—nevertheless, even the unhappy external condition of Florence Archer was no excuse. If she had truly loved her child, she could have brought an influence to bear upon him that would have saved him.

At college, Clarence found himself in a new world. At first, the reckless bearing and free conversation of some of the students surprised and shocked him. Soon, familiarity with such things made them seem less reprehensible. He could not only listen to them, but often join heartily in the laugh awakened by some sally of ribald wit. When alone, however, and the remembrance of home arose in his mind, he felt grieved to think that he could have taken pleasure in anything that would so have shocked his mother's ears.

He wrote home every week, and wrote with all the

frankness of a mind that had nothing to conceal. Every letter was promptly answered by his mother, and in every letter from her were some tenderly urged precepts that ever came with a timely force. These were not hackneyed repetitions of the same forms that had been enunciated time after time, until all their force was gone; nor did they come to her son in the shape of mere didactics. They had an appropriateness, a beauty, and a force about them, that ever inspired Clarence with a new love of what was morally excellent. If, at any time, he felt inclined to enter the forbidden grounds of pleasure, where too many of the students roved, the very next letter from home would win him back. The love of his mother was about him like a protecting sphere.

Very different was the case with James Fielding. It was not long before his natural love of companionship caused him to form intimate associations with several of the students whose principles and habits were not good. With these he spent hours every night in amusements and conversations by no means calculated to elevate the tone of his feelings. He made frequent efforts to induce Clarence to join them, who did so for a few times, but for a few times only. After having spent an evening in drinking, smoking, and card-playing, interspersed with songs and conversation such as his ears had never before heard, he found, on retiring to his room, a letter upon his table from his mother. The sight of this letter caused an instant revulsion in his feelings. He did not open it for some time. The very superscription, in the well-known hand-writing of his mother, seemed to rebuke him for having felt pleasure in what would have pained her pure mind deeply. When at length he opened and read the letter, it affected him to tears.

"My Dear Clarence,"—it said,—"How much we missed you last night at our family party. There were Marion, Henry, Fanny, and Lillian; but Clarence was away. I believe I thought much oftener of my absent one, than I did of those who were present. Henry accompanied Marion at the piano, on the flute, but not so perfectly as you used to do; and yet he plays very well for one so young. Fanny is improving rapidly in her music; she performed for us a very difficult overture, and did it exceedingly well. She dances, too, with admirable grace. How I wanted you to see her last evening. Dear little Lillian is always talking about you, and asking when you will come home. She grows sweeter and dearer every day. We had a very happy time, indeed, as we always have; but it would have been much happier, had not one been missing.

"I had a visit from Mrs. Fielding yesterday. She says that James has only written to her twice since he has been away. She asked me how often I heard from you; when I told her, every few days, she said that if she could hear from her boy every few weeks she would be very glad. Your mother thanks you, Clarence, for your promptness in writing. It is a great pleasure for me to hear from you often. How is James Fielding? Is he doing well? I wish he would write home more frequently. I thought his mother looked troubled when she spoke of him."

Clarence sighed and lifted his eyes from the letter on reading this passage. He thought of James Fielding, and the dangerous ground upon which he was standing, and sighed again as he resumed the perusal of his letter. The whole epistle came pure and true from a mother's heart, and it so filled the mind of Clarence with images of home, and made that home appear so like a little heaven, that he experienced a shuddering sensation when he compared with it the scene in which he had so lately been a participant.

"Thank God for such a mother!" he could not help ejaculating, as he read the last line of her letter. "Shall I ever cause her to shed a tear? No—never!"

When he met James Fielding next morning, he asked him—

"When did you hear from home, James?"

"From home? Oh, I'm sure I don't remember. I was going to say I don't hear from there at all; but I have had two letters from mother filling half a page each.

"When did you write?"

"About a month ago, to say I wanted some pocket-money."

"I heard from home last night."

"Ah! Got a remittance, I suppose?"

"Of love from my mother, more precious than gold or silver," replied Clarence with some feeling. "She says that your mother complains that you do not write to her."

"Say to your mother, **if you please,** that I complain **that my** mother doesn't write to me. So the account will stand balanced. I never could write a letter, except to say I wanted something. And I suppose mother is like me. We will excuse one another."

James spoke with a levity that pained Clarence. He wanted to admonish him, but felt that, in his present mood, it would be useless.

During the first year that Clarence was at college, the principles he had been taught by **his** mother became rules of action with him. He set his face resolutely against everything **that he** considered wrong. James Fielding, on the contrary, **was** among the most thoughtless young men in the institution. His wishes and passions were his rulers.

One day he came to Clarence and said,—

"There is to be some sport in about a week."

"Is there? What will it be like?"

"We don't intend going **to** morning prayers until seven o'clock."

" But the regulations say six."

" I know. Six is too early, and we are going to have it at seven."

" You did not come here to make laws, but to observe them," gravely replied Clarence.

" We came here to be instructed, not to be dragged out of bed to morning prayers before day—not to be bamboozled about by arbitrary Professors. It is a public institution, and the Faculty have no right to make oppressive laws."

"If any one dislikes these laws let him go home. It is the only honest course. But what else is intended ? "

" We intend——"

" *We !* Have you really joined in this conspiracy against law and order ? "

" Certainly I have. With the exception of about twenty, every student is pledged to go through with the matter when it is once started. My duty is to bring you over. We wish to rise as one man."

" After you have refused to attend morning prayers, what do you propose doing ? "

" If the hour is changed to seven, all well and good. Nothing more will be done ; but if not, our next course will be to attend regularly at six for a week, and scrape the chaplain down."

" What ? "

" Completely drown his voice by scraping our feet."

"You certainly are beside yourself, James. I cannot believe that *you* would join in doing so wrong a deed. In this you will not only insult the institution but Heaven."

"Oh, no. Heaven doesn't have much to do with the six o'clock prayers of college students."

"You speak with an unbecoming levity, James."

"Do I, indeed?" The lip of the boy slightly curled.

"What else is to be done?" asked Clarence, not noticing the manner of his companion.

"All sorts of things. Every regulation of the college is to be broken, unless our wishes are complied with. Wait a little, and you will see fun. But let me tell you—it is determined that every student who does not join us shall be dipped in the horse-pond. You had better consent. I should hate to see anything done to you."

The eyes of Clarence instantly flashed, and his cheeks grew as red as crimson.

"I would not consent if my life were taken," said the high-spirited boy. "But never fear. There is no one here that *dare* lay his hands upon me."

"Don't trust to that. There are those here who dare lay their hands upon anybody, and who will do it too. Come, then, say you will join us."

"No—never."

"You will be sorry when it is too late."

"I have no fears."

On the next day the matter was publicly broached during the college recess, when the students were alone.

"I move," said one, "that we begin on the morning after to-morrow."

"Second the motion," came from three or four voices.

"All who are in favour, hold up your hands."

More than a hundred hands were thrown into the air.

"All who are opposed will now hold up their hands."

A deep silence followed. Then a single hand was raised—then another, and another, until ten hands were seen above the heads of the crowd.—It was the hand of Clarence that first went up.

A murmur of discontent ran through the body of students, which deepened into execrations and threats. Half a dozen who were nearest Clarence gathered round him, with earnest and half angry remonstrances. His only reply was,—

"It is wrong, and I cannot join you."

"The regulation is oppressive," it was argued.

"Then leave the institution; but do not violate its laws."

"That is easily said; but others have a word in that as well as ourselves. All here are not exactly free to do as they please."

"It is better to endure what seems oppressive, than to do wrong."

"We don't mean to do wrong!" said several voices.

"You threaten to dip any one in the horse-pond who does not join you."

Several of the students looked confused, but one or two cried out,—

"Certainly we do; and what is more, our threats shall be executed."

"Right or wrong?" retorted Clarence, with a meaning look and voice, and, turning on his heel, walked away with a firm step.

His manner and words had their effect. He had said but little, but that little caused several who heard him to think more soberly. In nearly every little knot of students that was drawn together in the various rooms that night was one or more who had become lukewarm. A re-consideration of the matter was moved on the next day, and the question again taken. Instead of a dozen hands raised in the negative, as on the day before, there were now more than fifty. From that time little more was heard upon the subject. The revolt never took place.

So much for the influence of a single well-ordered, honest mind. Had the natural disposition of Clarence been unchecked, and had no counter-balancing principles been stored up in his mind, he would have been as eager for the proposed rebellion as the most thoughtless. What evil results might have followed cannot be told. There were those in the institution who did not love him much after this; but none who did not feel for him an involuntary respect.

CHAPTER X.

AN AGREEABLE SURPRISE.

THE incident just related occurred about a year and half after Clarence entered college. He had then nearly completed his sixteenth year.

About a week afterwards, and before they had received any communication from their son mentioning the circumstance, Mr. Hartley handed his wife a letter. Its contents were as follows:—

"Mr. James Hartley—

"DEAR SIR,—As the President of —— University, permit me to express to you my own and the thanks of the whole Faculty. The good and true principles which you have stored up in the mind of your son, have saved us from the evils of a well-planned resistance of authority by the students. No persuasions, we are told, could induce him to join with the rest. Personal violence was threatened, but this only made him adhere more firmly to his good resolution. The consequence was, that his conduct opened the eyes of one after another to see the folly of what they were about to do. Two parties were formed, and, before any overt act, the peace-party prevailed. We shall ever remember your son with admiration and gratitude. **From his** first entrance into our institution, he has been known **as** the strict observer **of all its rules,** and a diligent student. It is but just that his parents should **know all** this from **us.** With sentiments of the highest respect and regard,

   I am yours, &c.

    P—— R——,

      President of —— University."

Tears of **joy** gushed **to the eyes of** Mrs. Hartley as she finished the last line of this letter.

"Noble boy!" she said with enthusiasm.

"You are pleased with the letter then," **said her** husband, with assumed gravity.

"O yes! **Are you not?**" and she looked him in the face with surprise."

"Not exactly."

"Why?"

"It would have been all well enough, if the direction had not been wrong.

"What do **you** mean? Was it **not** *our* **son that** acted so nobly?"

"O yes. But the letter should have **been addressed** to you."

Mrs. Hartley smiled through her tears, and said,—

"It is all right.—Are we not one? But what would

my efforts have been without your wise counsel to second them. I will never care for the praise, so my boy does right. That is my sweetest reward. This is indeed a happy day. You know how much anxiety I have felt for Clarence. His peculiar temperament is, perhaps, the hardest there is to manage."

"And had you not been the most assiduous and wisest of mothers, you never could have moulded it into any form of beauty."

"Many an anxious day and sleepless night has it cost me. I sowed the seed in tears; but the dews of heaven watered the earth, and when the tender blade shot forth, the Sun of Righteousness warmed and strengthened it. Oh, how often have I felt discouraged! The selfishness of the boy was so strong, and he had so little regard for order. To counteract these, I laboured daily, and almost hourly. But I seemed to make little progress—sometimes all my efforts appeared fruitless. Still, I persevered, and it has not been in vain."

"Oh no. You have saved him from his worst enemy, himself."

"Henry is now old enough for college. What shall we do with him?" the mother said.

"Send him to —— University with his brother, I suppose. There is not a better institution in the country."

"Do you think it will be safe to send him from home?" asked Mrs. Hartley.

"Why not?"

"His disposition has changed little since he was a child. He is still confiding, and easily led away by others. Clarence had a strong will and prominent faults, which could be attacked vigorously; but the defects of Henry's character were hard to reach. I have thought much on the subject of sending him to college, but feel more and more reluctant to do so the nearer the time comes for making a decision on the subject."

"We ought not to deprive him of the advantages of a good education. He should stand side by side with his brother in this respect."

"True. But cannot we give him all these advantages at a less risk?"

"I know of no institution in this city where the same advantages may be secured as at ———."

"I believe there is none. But, should we look alone at this? Will our child be safe there? Is his character yet decided enough for us to trust him from our side? I think not. The frankness with which Clarence has written to us of the various temptations that have assailed him from time to time, has opened my eyes to the dangers that must encompass a boy like Henry in such a place. I should not feel happy a moment were he to go there."

"Then he must not go," said Mr. Hartley, firmly. "You have ever been a true mother to our children.

and your love has thus far led you to determine wisely in regard to them. Though I must own that I feel very reluctant to deprive the boy of the advantages of a thorough college course of instruction."

"Have not my reasons force in your mind?" asked Mrs. Hartley. "Do you not believe that it would be wrong for us to jeopardize the spiritual interests of our child, in the eager pursuit of intellectual advantages?"

"I certainly do; the latter should only be for the sake of the former. The intellect should be cultivated as the means of developing the moral powers, that both in union may act in life with true efficiency. If all the higher objects of education can be secured by keeping our child at home, we ought not, under any circumstances, to send him away."

"They may often be better secured away from home, if the boy have firmness enough to resist the temptations that will assail him; but the question, whether the boy can so resist, must be decided by the parents before he is sent out to make his first trial on the world-arena."

"My own feeling is, that we had better keep Henry under our guidance as long as it can be done. He is not a boy with the quick intellect of Clarence, and will probably never be ambitious to move in a sphere where the highest attainments are required. It would be much more agreeable to him now to go to work in your warehouse than to go to school."

"And I shall not grieve over his choice of a pursuit in life, if he should prefer the calling of a merchant."

"Nor I. Active employment is the best for all; and in choosing a profession in life, that should always be chosen which will give the mind great activity, while, at the same time, it brings in the affections also. The pursuit of any calling which a man does not like, can never result to his own and the public advantage in so high a degree as it would were his heart in what he was doing. For this reason, we ought to be governed very much, in deciding for our children, by their fitness for and preference for a pursuit in business."

"Children's preferences, however, do not always arise from any peculiar fitness in themselves, but often from caprice."

"It is the business of a wise parent to discriminate between a natural fitness for a thing, and a fleeting preference for it. The imagination of young persons is very active, and apt to throw a false light around that upon which it dwells."

Many conversations of a like nature were held by Mr. and Mrs. Hartley, who finally came to the determination to keep Henry at home. The boy was disappointed at this. He wanted to go to college; not, the parents could easily enough see, for the sake of the superior advantages there to be obtained, but because his imagination had thrown a peculiar charm about a college life.

Before making a final decision on the subject, Mrs. Hartley thought it right to bring Clarence into their confidence. She wrote him a long letter on the subject, and asked him to give his opinion of the effect that would be produced upon a boy like Henry, if introduced among the students. "You know his disposition," she said, "and how he would be affected by the kind of associations into which he would be thrown."

Clarence wrote back immediately that he did not believe it would be good for Henry to be exposed to the temptations of a college life. "He is too easily led away by others," he remarked. "I have noticed more than a dozen instances, since I have been here, of boys just like Henry, who were innocent and confiding in their dispositions when they came, who soon became so changed that it made me sad to think about it. There was one boy in particular. His mother came with him when he first entered college. She appeared to be deeply attached to him, and he to her—they both wept bitterly at parting. She was a widow, and he her only remaining child, upon whom all her care, affection, and pride were lavished. He soon made friends, for all seemed drawn towards him. Singular as it may seem, the boy, between whom and himself the warmest attachment arose, was as unlike him as it is possible to imagine. He was a bold, bad boy—full of life, and ready to do almost anything that a reckless spirit prompted. In a little while they were inseparable companions. At the end of six months, the spirit of the one seemed to have been transfused into that of the other. I almost wonder, sometimes, if the mother would know her son were they to meet unexpectedly. I hope you will not send Henry here. He might pass through his course uncontaminated, but I think it would be dangerous to expose one like him to so many temptations."

This letter fully decided Mr. and Mrs. Hartley.

CHAPTER XI.

GOING INTO COMPANY.

MARION was in her eighteenth year, and yet she had been taken into company by her parents but very little. Her virtues were all of a domestic character, and graced the home circle. She knew of little beyond its pleasant precincts. Few who saw her supposed that she was more than fifteen years of age. Not that her mind was unmatured, but because her appearance was girlish, and her manners simple and unaffected, yet retiring when strangers were present.

"How old is Marion?" asked Mrs. Fielding, who had called in one morning to chat away half an hour with Mrs. Hartley. Marion had just left the room.

"In her eighteenth year," was replied.

"Nearly eighteen! Surely it cannot be."

"Yes. That is her age."

"I never would have believed it. Why, she looks more like a girl of thirteen or fourteen."

"I don't know. She doesn't seem so very young to me."

"But why in the world do you keep the poor thing back so? She should have been introduced into company two years ago. I had no idea that she was so old."

Mrs. Fielding had a daughter only in her seventeenth year, who had been flourishing about at all the balls and parties for the past two seasons, and had now all the silly airs and affectations which a young miss, under such circumstances, might be expected to acquire. Jane Fielding had met Marion several times, on calling at Mrs. Hartley's with her mother, but, imagining her to be a mere child, in comparison with herself, she had treated her as such. Marion was never pushed forward by her mother, and, therefore, the mistake of Mrs. Fielding and her daughter was not corrected by their own observation.

"There is plenty of time yet," said Mrs. Hartley, in reply to the remark of her visitor. "Ten young ladies go into company too early, where one goes in too late."

"I doubt that. If you don't take your daughter into polished society early, she will never acquire that grace and ease of manner so beautiful and so essential."

Involuntarily did Mrs. Hartley compare, **in her own mind**, the forward, chattering, flirting Jane Fielding with her own modest child, in whom all the graces of a sweet spirit shone with a tempered yet beautiful lustre.

"I am more anxious that my daughter shall be a true woman, when she arrives **at** woman's age, than an artificial woman, **while a mere child,"** she could not help replying.

"**A** very strange remark," said Mrs. Fielding.

"And yet it expresses my views on the subject."

"I should hardly think you had reflected much about it, and was merely acting from some antiquated notion put into your head by Aunt Mary."

"You err there **very much, Mrs.** Fielding. **Since** the birth of **my** daughter, the attainment of the best means for securing her happiness has been with me a source of deep reflection. I have brought to my aid the observations of my youth and mature years. **What** I have seen in real life confirms my rational deductions. I am well satisfied that it injures a young girl to throw her into company early. It is from this conviction that I act."

"How **can** it injure her? I am at a loss to know."

"It injures her in everything, I was going to say."

"Name a single particular."

"It puts a woman's head upon a girl's shoulders, to use a common saying, while she lacks the strength to carry it steadily, but tosses the feathers with which it is dressed into every body's face that she meets."

"O dear! What a queer idea!"

"And not only that, Mrs. Fielding; it exposes her, before she has the intelligence to discriminate accurately between the true and the false, to the danger of forming a wrong estimate of life and its duties—of being carried away by a love of dress, and show, and mere pleasure-taking, while things of infinitely more importance are seen in an obscure light, and viewed as of little consequence. The manners of a girl who has gone into company too early are always offensive to me. There is a pertness about her I cannot bear—a toss of the head, a motion of the body, an affected distortion of the countenance—(I can call it nothing else)—that is peculiarly disagreeable."

"You see a great deal more than I do, that is all I can say, Mrs. Hartley;" replied Mrs. Fielding, a little gravely. She had that very morning felt called upon to rebuke Jane for the rude forwardness of her manners in company the evening previous!

"Perhaps I have thought more on the subject, and, in consequence, observed more closely."

"I don't know how that is—perhaps so,"—was the visitor's rather cold reply.

A new subject of conversation was then started.

While they still sat conversing, Marion, who had gone out to attend to something, came in with little Lillian by the hand, now just five years old. Mrs. Fielding looked into her face with a new interest, observed her words closely, and watched every motion. Involuntary respect, and even admiration, were elicited. There was something innocent and like a child about her, and yet this was so blended with a womanly grace when she conversed, that, in spite of herself, she could not help contrasting her manner with the forward, familiar airs of her own daughter.

Mrs. Hartley's visitor did not feel very well pleased with herself or her daughter for some days after this conversation. There was so much of truth about what had been said, and truth bearing upon her own conduct as a mother, that it made her uncomfortable. But it was too late for her to mend—the evil was already done. The more she thought about the picture Mrs. Hartley had drawn of a puppet-woman, as she had chosen to call her, the more closely did she perceive that her own daughter resembled the sketch, until she felt half angry at what appeared almost too pointed an allusion.

The next time that Mrs. Fielding and her daughter called upon Mrs. Hartley, the latter paid a much more respectful attention to Marion than she had ever before done. She was surprised to find, in one she had looked upon as a girl too young for her to associate with, a quiet dignity of manner and womanly tone of character beyond what she had supposed to exist. At first she rattled on with her in quite a patronizing way, but before she left she was rather inclined to listen than to talk.

"While our mammas are talking, let us have some music," Jane said, during a pause in the conversation. "Are you fond of playing?"

"I am fond of music, and always like good playing. Come to the piano—you play well, I understand. I shall enjoy your performance very much."

Jane sat down to the piano, and rattled off several fashionable frivolities, in a kind of hap-hazard style. Marion was disappointed, and did not, for she could not, praise the young lady's playing. She had learned only to speak what she thought, and when she could not praise, and utter the truth, she said nothing.

"Play something else," she said.

Jane turned over the music books and selected an overture that required a brilliant performer to execute it with anything like its true effect. On this she went to work with might and main, and got through it in about ten minutes, much to the relief of Marion, whose fine perception of musical harmonies was terribly outraged.

"Now *you* must play," said Jane, as she struck the last note, rising from the instrument.

Marion sat down and let her fingers fall upon the

keys, that answered to their touch as if half conscious.

"You play indeed!" exclaimed Jane, after Marion had played a short piece of music with fine taste. "Do you sing?"

"Sometimes."

"Can you sing 'The Banks of the Blue Moselle?'"

"I believe so." Marion ran her fingers over the keys, and then warbled that sprightly song in a low, sweet voice, that really charmed her companion. The ease with which this was done surprised Jane. It seemed to cost Marion scarce an effort. Half a dozen other songs were named, and sung by Marion, who then asked Jane if she would not sing.

"Not after you," replied the young lady, taking a step back from the piano.

Marion did not know how to reply to such a remark, and so she said nothing. She could not lavish false compliments, nor did she wish to make any allusion to her own performance. She had sung to please her visitor, and had not a thought beyond that.

Mrs. Fielding was less self-satisfied than ever after this visit. She could not but acknowledge to herself, that she would much rather her daughter were more like Marion.

CHAPTER XII.

A PAINFUL BEREAVEMENT.

Thus far in her maternal life, Mrs. Hartley had endured all the pains, cares, anxieties, hopes, and fears, of a mother, but neither sorrow nor bereavement. Her assiduous care had, thus far, been rewarded by the very best results. But now there came a heart-searching trial, which no act of hers could possibly prevent.

On the day that Mrs. Fielding and her daughter called upon Mrs. Hartley, Lillian did not seem very well. She drooped about, and was very fretful, a thing with her very unusual. At night she dropped off to sleep an hour earlier than usual. When Mr. Hartley came home, and inquired for his little pet, he was told that she was in bed. He loved the child with great tenderness, and missed her bright face and merry voice. Taking up a light, he went to the chamber where she slept, and stood over her little bed for some time, looking down upon her sweet face. While doing so, Mrs. Hartley joined him.

"Dear little thing," she said, "she has not appeared well all day."

The father placed his hand upon her forehead.

"Why, Anna," he said, "she has a high fever! And listen! how hard she breathes."

Mrs. Hartley laid her hands upon the child's cheek

with a feeling of uneasiness. Her children had often been sick with fevers; but never, in the incipient stage of the disease, had she felt the peculiar sensation of uneasiness and oppression that followed the discovery that Lillian was really sick.

In a little while the tea bell rang, and the family gathered around the table to partake of their evening meal. The father and mother felt no appetite, and merely sipped their tea. Marion was silent from some cause. Henry and Fanny were the only ones who had anything to say. On rising from the table, Mr. and Mrs. Hartley repaired to the chamber to look at Lillian again. The child's fever seemed higher, and she had become restless. She coughed occasionally, and there was much oppression on her chest.

"I think we had better call in the doctor," said Mr. Hartley.

"It may only be a temporary indisposition, that will subside before morning," remarked the mother.

"Still it is better to be frightened than hurt," returned Mr. Hartley.

"True. But suppose we wait for an hour."

At the expiration of an hour the child was no better. A physician was called in, who gave some simple medicine, and said he would call in the morning. The morning found the child very ill. What form the disease would ultimately assume, the doctor could not tell;—it might only be a violent catarrh, it might be some more malignant disease. A sudden gloom **fell over the whole household, such as had never been felt before.** The mother could not compose herself to do anything—Marion sat by the child's bedside nearly all the time, and Mr. Hartley came home two or three times during the day. What alarmed them most of all was the constant complaints of Lillian that her throat pained her, and the admission of the **doctor** that it was highly inflamed. Even hours before **the** physician declared the disease to be scarlet fever, they were more than half assured that it was nothing else.

On the third day, all their fears were confirmed. The disease began to assume its worst type. The skin was red and tumefied, **the** throat badly ulcerated, and the face much swollen. **Breathing was exceedingly** difficult, and there was an eruption of dark scarlet spots on the face, neck, and chest. On the fifth day, the little sufferer became delirious—on the seventh day she was freed from her pain. Her spirit returned to the God who gave it.

Suddenly as this terrible affliction had fallen upon them, in the brief space that ensued between the illness of the child and her removal, the minds of the parents had become, in some degree, prepared for the result that followed. Still the blow stunned them, and it was not until called upon to take the last look at their little one, and to touch with their lips for the last time **her** snowy forehead, that they realized the full consciousness of what they had lost. Ah! who but they who love tenderly a sweet, innocent, affectionate child, can understand how deep was the anguish of their spirits at the moment when they turned away after taking their last, lingering look at the marble features of their departed Lillian.

How desolate seemed every part of the house for days afterwards. Hard as the mother tried to bear up and to look up in this affliction, she had not the power to dry her tears. For hours, sometimes, she would sit in dreamy absence of mind, all interest in things surrounding her having totally subsided.

"Dear Anna," her husband ventured to say to her one day, when he came home and found her in this state, "Time, the Restorer, cannot do his work for us, unless we do our part. You remember Dr. T——, in whose family we spent two pleasant weeks last summer. He had a son just about the age of Clarence—perhaps two years older—who had just passed through his collegiate course with distinguished honours. The doctor loved that boy with more than ordinary tenderness. 'He was always a good boy,' he said to me, in alluding to his son. 'His love of truth was strong, and his sense of honour most acute. I not only loved him, but I was proud of him.' This son had not been home long when he became ill and died. 'I never had anything in my whole life that gave me such anguish of spirit as the death of that boy,' he said, and his voice even then trembled. 'But, through the whole painful scene of sickness, death, and burial, I never missed a patient. I knew that there was only one thing that would sustain me in my affliction, and that was, the steady and faithful performance of my regular duties in life. But for this, I sometimes think I could not have borne the weight that was then laid upon me.' Dear Anna! Doctor T—— was a true philosopher; for his was a high Christian philosophy, that sought relief from affliction in the performance of duty to others."

Poor Mrs. Hartley wept bitterly while her husband was speaking; but his words sunk into her heart, and she felt that she was suffering severer pain than would have been her portion if she had acted like Dr. T——. From that time she strove with a great effort to arouse herself from the dreamy state into which she had fallen. It was difficult to perform all the duties—nay, she could not perform them all—that heretofore claimed her attention. For five years her daily thought and care had been for her youngest born, the nursling of the flock, and now she was taken away. For a time she struggled to act upon her husband's suggestion, but again sunk down; and efforts to elevate her from this state of gloomy depression were again made. She lay weeping, with her head upon her husband's bosom, one night, when he said,—

"Anna, dear, would you like to have Lillian back again?"

She did not reply, but sobbed more violently for nearly a minute, and then grew calm. Her husband repeated his inquiry.

"I have never asked myself that question," she answered.

"Think now, and determine in your own mind, whether, if you had the power to recall her, you would do so."

"I do not think I would," was murmured half reluctantly.

"Why not?"

"It is better for her to remain where she is."

"Do you really think so?"

"How can you ask such a question? Is she not now safe in her heavenly home? Is she not loved and cared for by Jesus? She can have no pain nor grief where she is gone. She has escaped a life of trial and sorrow. Ah, my dear husband, even in my affliction I can say, I am thankful that, with her, life's toilsome journey is over—that her probation has been short."

"Spoken like my own dear wife," Mr. Hartley said with emotion. "I, too, grieve over the loss, with a grief that words cannot express, but I would not take back the treasure now safely laid up in heaven. She cannot return to us, but we shall go to her. Our real home is not here. A short time before us has our child gone; we shall soon follow after, but not until all the duties we owe to others are paid. We have still four left, and, do our best, we cannot do too much for them."

"Too much! Oh, no! my constant regret is that I do too little. And now that Lillian has been taken away, I seem to have lost the power to do even that little."

"Strive to think more of those that are left than of the one that is gone. No effort of yours can do her any good, but every effort you make for those that still remain will add to their happiness. Yesterday, when I came home, I found Fanny sitting alone in the parlour. She looked very sad. 'What is the matter, dear?' I asked. 'Mother cries so, and don't talk to me as she did,' she said, the tears coming into her dear little eyes."

"O James! did she say that?"

"Yes, dear. And if you could have seen her face, and heard the tone of her voice, you would have grieved to think how sad the child's heart must be. She, as well as the rest of us, has lost much in the death of Lillian. You know how much she loved the child."

"And I," sobbed the mother, "have left her to bear her grief alone. Alas! how selfish I have been in my sorrow. But it shall no longer be. I will meet my children as a mother should meet them. I will help them to bear their loss."

Mrs. Hartley met her family on the next morning

with a calmer **brow**. She had a word for each; and that word was spoken with an unusual tenderness of expression. Fanny looked earnestly into her mother's face, when she observed the change, **and drew close up** to her side.

"You love me, dear mother, don't you?" **whispered** the child, close to her ear.

"Love you, my child! Oh, yes! A thousand times more than I can **tell**." And she kissed her fervently.

"And the angels in heaven love Lillian, don't they?"

"Yes, love," Mrs. Hartley replied, in a husky whisper, struggling to keep the tears from gushing from her eyes.

"I know the good angels will love **her**, and **take** care of her just as well as you did, mother."

"Oh, yes! and a great deal **better**."

"Then we won't cry any more because she is gone."

"Not if we can help it, love. But we miss her very much."

"Yes. I want to see her all the time. But I know she is in heaven, and I won't cry for her to come back."

The words of Fanny were near effecting the entire overthrow of Mrs. Hartley's feelings; but by a vigorous struggle with herself, she remained calm, and continued for some time to talk with the child about Lillian in heaven.

From this period, the mother's love for her children

flowed on again in its wonted channels, and her care for them was as assiduous as ever. In fact, the loss of one caused her to draw her arms more closely about the rest. But she was changed; and no one who looked upon her could help noting the change. The quiet thoughtfulness of her countenance had given place to a musing expression, as if she were, in spirit, far away with some dearly loved object. Although her love for her children, and her anxiety for their welfare, was increased, if there was any change, yet that love was more brooding than active in its nature. The creative energy of her mind appeared to have suffered a slight paralysis. The bow was unbent. Marion was quick to perceive this, and by the intuition of love, to glide almost insensibly into her mother's place, so far as Henry and Fanny were concerned. The groundwork of home-education had been so well laid by the mother, that the sister's task was not a difficult one. She became Henry's confidante and counsellor, and led Fanny gently on in the acquirement of good habits and good principles.

If to no one else, this change was good for Marion. It gave her objects to love intensely, because their well-being depended on her conduct towards them, at an age when the heart needs something upon which to lavish the pure waters of affection that begin to flow forth in gushing profusion.

Another effect was, to make more distant the period

when Marion should appear upon the stage of life as a woman; and this was no wrong to the sweet maiden. When she did enter society as a woman, she was a woman fully qualified to act her part with wisdom and prudence.

CHAPTER XIII.

AN IMPORTANT ERA IN LIFE.

WHEN Clarence returned from college, unscathed in the ordeal through which he had passed, he entered upon a course of legal studies. Law was the profession he chose. It most frequently happens that brothers, as they approach manhood, do not become intimate as companions. But it was not so in the case of Clarence and Henry. They were drawn together as soon as the former returned home. This again tended to lessen the care of Mrs. Hartley, for Clarence had become, in one sense, his brother's guardian. Instead, now, of the constant and often intense exercise of mind to which she had been subjected for years, in the determination of what course was best to take with her children, in order to secure their greatest good, she was more their pleasant companion than their mentor. Her aim now was to secure their unlimited confidence, and this she was able to do. Their mistakes were never treated with even playful ridicule;

but she sympathized earnestly with them in everything that interested their minds. This led them to talk to her with the utmost freedom, and gave her a knowledge of the exact state of their feelings in regard to all the circumstances that transpired around them.

The completion of Clarence's twenty-first year was a period to which both the son and mother had looked with no ordinary interest—but with very different feelings. So important an era Mrs. Hartley could **not** let pass without a long and serious conversation with her son, or rather repeated conversations with him.

"From this time, my son," she said to him, "you are no **longer** bound to your parents by the law of obedience. **You are a man, and** must act in freedom, according to reason. Our **precepts are not to be** observed *because* we give them, but are to be observed because you see them to be true. Heretofore, your parents have been responsible for your conduct to society. But now, you alone are responsible. Upon the **way in** which you exercise the freedom you now enjoy will depend your usefulness as a man, and your eternal state hereafter. Choose, my son, with wisdom —let your paths be those of peace and pleasantness."

"Don't say your work is ended, my mother," Clarence said with much feeling, and an expression of deep concern upon his face. "It cannot be. As before, **your** advice and counsel must be good. I will not believe that I am no longer to obey you—O no! no!"

"In a supreme sense, Clarence, the Lord is your father, and to him alone are you now required to give supreme obedience, and to love with your highest, purest, and best affections. But that need not cause you to love your natural father and mother the less. You say truly, that our work is not yet done. Our counsel will still be given, but you must not follow it because we have given it, but because, in the light of your own mind, you perceive that it accords with the truth ; for you must never forget, that according to your *own* deeds will you be justified or condemned. We shall not love you the less, nor be less anxious for your welfare; but, being a man, you must act as a man, in freedom according to reason."

The recollection of this conversation often **made** Clarence sigh. "Ah!" he would sometimes say to himself,—"man's estate **is not,** after all, so desirable a thing to attain. It was much easier to lie upon my mother's bosom, than it is to fight my way through life, amid its thousand temptations."

The formal and serious manner in which **Mrs.** Hartley had conversed with Clarence, caused all that she said to be deeply impressed upon his mind. He pondered over it for weeks. The effect was good, for it saved him from the thoughtless tendency of mere pleasure-seeking into which young men are too apt to fall, on finding themselves entirely free from the shackles of minority. He saw clearly and felt strongly the responsibility of his position. But, accompanying this perception, was an earnestly formed resolution to overcome in every temptation that might assail him.

"I can conquer, and I will," he said, in the confidence that he felt in the more than human strength that those receive who fight against evil.

It was not long before life's conflicts began in earnest with him; but it is not our business to speak of them, further than to say, that he was subjected to strong trials, to severe temptations, to cares and anxieties of no ordinary kind, and that the remains of good and truth stored up in his mind by his mother saved him. As a child, his predominant evil qualities were a strong self-will and extreme selfishness. In manhood, they reappeared, and long and intense was the struggle against them, before they yielded themselves subject to more heavenly principles.

CHAPTER XIV.

HAPPY CONSUMMATIONS.

MARION HARTLEY was twenty-two years of age when she first began to attract attention in society. The impression she made was a decided one. People talked about her for a time as a new wonder. Her grace, her intelligence, her accomplishments, and, not least, her beauty, won universal admiration. She was quickly surrounded by the butterflies of fashion, but they found themselves at a loss how to be truly agreeable. If they flattered her, she did not seem to understand them; if they complimented her upon her singing or dancing, she only smiled quietly. In fact, all their usual arts failed. Some called her cold—others said she was as proud as a duchess; while others reported that her heart was engaged to an absent lover.

Unconscious of all this agitation created by her appearance, Marion continued in the affectionate performance of her home duties, occasionally mingling in society, less from feeling drawn thither than because she believed she owed something to the social as well as to the family circle.

Once more was the liveliest maternal interest awakened in the bosom of Mrs. Hartley. Now was the most critical period in her daughter's life. Her heart could not long remain uninterested; but whose hand should touch the precious fountain, and unseal its pure waters? That was the anxious question.

Evening visitors were becoming more and more frequent. On every new appearance of Marion in company would some new acquaintance call. Mr. and Mrs. Hartley, unlike most parents, who, very considerately remembering how it was with themselves, "leave the young people alone," always made it a point to be present, with other members of the family, when any visitor called to spend an evening. Clarence, who was fully in his mother's confidence, remained at home a great deal during these occasions, in order to swell the parlour circle, and to add to the pleasures of conversation, music, or other modes that might be resorted to for passing an hour.

This way of doing things was not at all relished by some who were all eagerness to secure the favour of Marion. Among those who occasionally dropped in, was a young man who generally spent more time in conversing with the mother than with the daughter. If his design had been first to conciliate Mrs. Hartley, his plan was certainly a good one. But he was innocent of any further design than to gain opportunities for observing closely the character and disposition of Marion. He had ample means for supporting a wife, and had been looking about him for one at least a year. The first impression made upon him by Marion was favourable. He was not struck by her beauty and accomplishments half so much as by the sentiments which he occasionally heard fall from her lips. The way in which her parents guarded her, he saw and understood at once, and this strengthened his belief that she was a precious treasure for him who could win her heart.

While he observed her at a distance, as it were, others were clustering around her, and using every art to gain her favour. But, even while they were pressing for attention, her eye was wandering away to him, and often the words they uttered were unheard in her recollection of sentiments which he had spoken. Why this was so, Marion did not ask herself. She did not even notice the fact. When the young man at last began to make advances, she received them with an inward pleasure unfelt before. This did not escape the mother's watchful eye; but she had no word to say in objection. Long before any serious inroad upon Marion's affections had been made, father, mother, and brother were thoroughly acquainted with the young man's family, standing, and character. They were unexceptionable.

When he finally made application for her hand, he received promptly this answer:—

"Take her, and may she be to you as good **a** wife **as** she has been to us a child."

Marion was twenty-three **years of** age when she became a wedded wife. Many wed younger, but few as wisely.

The next event of interest in the life of Mrs. Hartley was the marriage of Clarence. In this matter she was careful to leave her son in the most perfect freedom. Although from principle she did this, she was not without great concern on the subject; for she well knew that his whole character would be modified for good and evil by his wife. It is enough to say that Clarence chose wisely.

CHAPTER XV.

CONCLUSION.

Having brought our readers to this point, not, we hope, without profit to themselves, we find that we have little more to add. The mother's untiring devotion to her children has not been in vain. The good seed sown in their minds has produced a pleasant harvest.

We could present a strong and painful contrast in the results attendant upon the course pursued by Mrs. Fielding; but we will not do so. It would be of little use to throw dark shades upon the picture we have drawn. There are few who read this, who cannot look around and see the baleful consequences that have followed neglect and indifference such as were manifested by Mrs. Fielding towards her children. The instances are, alas! too numerous.

In closing this volume, the author would remark to those who may feel disappointed in not finding it so full of incident and description as they had expected, that to have given it a lighter character would have required the sacrifice of much that he wished to say. The subject is one so full of interest to a certain class, that no charms of fiction were required to hold their attention. To have extended our book further, or to have introduced a greater variety of scenes, would have occupied the time and attention of the reader to very little purpose. To those who have read aright, enough has been said—volumes would do no good to those who have not.

Art Gift-Books.

An entirely New Series of First-Class and richly Illustrated Books on Nature and Natural History.

NEW VOLUME.

The Insect. By Jules Michelet, Author of "History of France," "The Bird," &c. With One Hundred and Forty Illustrations drawn specially for this Edition by GIACOMELLI, and engraved by the most eminent French and English Artists. Imperial 8vo, cloth, richly gilt. Price 10s. 6d.

Nature; or, The Poetry of Earth and Sea. From the French of MME. MICHELET. With upwards of Two Hundred Illustrations drawn specially for this Work by GIACOMELLI (Illustrator of "The Bird"), and engraved by the most eminent French and English Artists. Imperial 8vo, cloth, richly gilt. Price 10s. 6d.

The Mountain. From the French of Jules MICHELET, Author of "The Bird," &c. With upwards of Sixty Illustrations by PERCIVAL SKELTON and CLARK STANTON. Imperial 8vo, cloth, richly gilt. Price 10s. 6d.

The Bird. By Jules Michelet, Author of "History of France," &c. Illustrated by Two Hundred and Ten Exquisite Engravings by GIACOMELLI. Imperial 8vo, full gilt side and gilt edges. Price 10s. 6d.

The Mysteries of the Ocean. By Arthur MANGIN. With One Hundred and Thirty Illustrations by W. FREEMAN and J. NOEL. Imperial 8vo, full gilt side and gilt edges. Price 10s. 6d.

The Sea. By Jules Michelet, Author of "The Bird," "The Insect," &c. With Nine Tinted Engravings. Imperial 8vo, cloth, richly gilt. Price 10s. 6d.

Earth and Sea. By Louis Figuier. With Two Hundred and Fifty Engravings. Imperial 8vo, handsomely bound in cloth and gold. Price 10s. 6d.

T. NELSON AND SONS, LONDON, EDINBURGH, AND NEW YORK

Travel and Research
IN BIBLE LANDS.

The Land and the Book; or, Biblical Illustrations Drawn from the Manners and Customs, the Scenes and Scenery of the Holy Land. By the Rev. W. M. THOMSON, D.D. Crown 8vo, 718 pages, with Twelve Coloured Illustrations and One Hundred and Twenty Woodcuts. Price 7s. 6d., cloth; morocco, 15s.

In the Holy Land. By the Rev. Andrew THOMSON, D.D., Edinburgh, Author of "Great Missionaries." With Eighteen Engravings. Crown 8vo, cloth extra. Price 6s. 6d.

Bashan's Giant Cities and Syria's Holy Places. By Professor PORTER, Author of "Murray's Hand-book to Syria and Palestine." With Eight Beautiful Engravings. Post 8vo, cloth extra. Price 7s. 6d.

Ruined Cities of Bible Lands. By the late Rev. W. K. TWEEDIE, D.D. With Tinted Frontispiece and Vignette, and Sixty Engravings. Foolscap 8vo, cloth. Price 2s.

THE HOLY LAND—DESCRIBED AND ILLUSTRATED.
Illuminated Side, cloth extra. Price 1s. 6d. each.

Jerusalem: Pictorial and Descriptive. By the late Rev. W. K. TWEEDIE, D.D. With Seventy Engravings.

The Environs of Jerusalem: Pictorial and Descriptive. With Fifty Woodcuts.

The Jordan and its Valley, and the Dead Sea. With Fifty Woodcuts.

The Fall of Jerusalem; and the Roman Conquest of Judea. With Fifty Woodcuts.

T. NELSON AND SONS, LONDON, EDINBURGH, AND NEW YORK.

Art Gift-Books.

The History **of** the Robins. **By** Mrs. Trimmer. With Seventy Original Drawings by GIACOMELLI, engraved by Rouget, Berveiller, Whymper, Sargent, and Morison. Small 4to, cloth, full gilt. Price 6s. 6d.

Poems **of** Natural History for the Young. By MARY HOWITT. Illustrated with Coloured Frontispiece and Illuminated Title-page, and upwards of One Hundred Drawings by GIACOMELLI, Illustrator of "The Bird" by Michelet. Small 4to, cloth, richly gilt. Price 6s.

Birds and Flowers, and Other Country Things. By MARY HOWITT. Illustrated with Coloured Frontispiece and Illuminated Title-page, and upwards of One Hundred Drawings by GIACOMELLI. Small 4to, cloth, richly gilt. Price 6s.

The **W**orld at Home: Pictures and Scenes from Far-off Lands. By MARY and ELIZABETH KIRBY. With upwards of One Hundred and Thirty Illustrations. Small 4to, cloth, **richly** gilt. Price 6s.

The **Sea** and its Wonders. By Mary and ELIZABETH KIRBY. With One Hundred and Seventy-four Illustrations. **Small 4to, cloth, richly** gilt. **Price 6s.**

Works on Natural History.

Animal Life throughout the Globe. An Illustrated **Book** of Natural History. With Two Hundred **and Thirty-six** Engravings. Crown 8vo, cloth extra. **Price 6s., plain edges;** or, 6s. 6d., gilt edges.

Beautiful Birds **in** Far-off Lands: Their Haunts and Homes. **By** MARY and ELIZABETH KIRBY, Authors of "The W**orld** at Home," &c. With Sixteen exquisitely Coloured Illustrations. Crown 8vo, cloth extra. 5s.

The Monsters of the Deep, and Curiosities of Ocean Life. A Book of Anecdotes, Traditions, and Legends. With upwards of Seventy Engravings. Post 8vo, cloth extra. Price 3s. 6d.

Stories of Bird Life: A Book of Facts **and** Anecdotes Illustrative of the Habits and Intelligence of the Feathered Tribes. By HENRY BERTHOUD. With One Hundred Illustrations. Post 8vo, cloth extra. Price 3s. 6d.

Illustrated Books of Science and History.

Lighthouses and Lightships: A Descriptive and Historical Account of their Mode of Construction and Organization. By W. H. DAVENPORT ADAMS. With Seventy Illustrations from Photographs and other Sources. Post 8vo, cloth extra. Price 3s. 6d.

Life in the Primeval World. Founded on Meunier's "Les Animaux d'Autrefois." By W. H. DAVENPORT ADAMS. With Eighty-nine Engravings. Post 8vo, cloth. Price 2s. 6d.

Earth and its Treasures: A Description of the Metallic and Mineral Wealth of Nature. By ARTHUR MANGIN, Author of "The Desert World," &c. Edited by W. H. DAVENPORT ADAMS. With Fifty Engravings. Post 8vo, cloth extra. Price 3s. 6d.

The Glacier, the Iceberg, the Ice-field, and the Avalanche. With Seventy Engravings. Post 8vo, cloth extra. Price 3s. 6d.

Maury's Physical Geography of the Sea. With Thirteen Charts printed in Colours. 8vo, cloth. Price 5s.

Beneath the Surface; or, The Wonders of the Underground World. By W. H. DAVENPORT ADAMS. With One Hundred and Fifteen Engravings. Post 8vo, cloth extra. Price 3s. 6d.

The Treasures of the Deep; or, A Descriptive Account of the Great Fisheries, and their Products. With numerous Engravings. Post 8vo, cloth extra. Price 3s. 6d.

The Buried Cities of Campania; or, Pompeii and Herculaneum: Their History, their Destruction, and their Remains. By W. H. DAVENPORT ADAMS. With Fifty-seven Engravings and a Plan of Pompeii. Post 8vo, cloth extra. Price 3s.

The Queen of the Adriatic; or, Venice Past and Present. By W. H. DAVENPORT ADAMS. With Thirty-one Engravings. Post 8vo, cloth. Price 3s.

Triumphs of Invention and Discovery. By J. H. FYFE. New Edition. With Seven Engravings. Post 8vo, cloth. Price 2s. 6d.

Gaussen's World's Birthday. Illustrated. Foolscap 8vo, cloth. Price 2s. 6d.

T. NELSON AND SONS, LONDON, EDINBURGH, AND NEW YORK.

Recent Publications.

The Haunted Room. A Tale. By A. L. O. E.
Post 8vo, cloth. Price 3s. 6d.

Little Hazel, the King's Messenger. By the Author of "Little Snowdrop and her Golden Casket," &c. With Coloured Frontispiece and Vignette Title. Post 8vo, cloth extra. Price 2s. 6d.

Under the Old Oaks; or, Won by Love. By the Author of "Little Hazel, the King's Messenger," &c. With Coloured Frontispiece and Vignette Title. Post 8vo, cloth extra. Price 2s. 6d.

After Many Days; or, Clear Shining after Rain. With Four Illustrations printed in Colours. Post 8vo, cloth extra. Price 2s. 6d.

Leonie; or, Light Out of Darkness: and Within Iron Walls, a Tale of the Siege of Paris. Twin Stories of the Franco-German War. By ANNIE LUCAS. Crown 8vo, cloth extra. Price 6s. 6d.

Herman; or, The Little Preacher: Little Threads: and, The Story Lizzie Told. By the Author of "Stepping Heavenward," "Little Susy's Six Birthdays," &c. With Four Illustrations printed in Colours. Post 8vo, cloth extra. Price 2s. 6d.

Lizzie Hepburn; or, Every Cloud has a Silver Lining. With Four Illustrations printed in Colours. Post 8vo, cloth extra. Price 2s. 6d.

Little Snowdrop and her Golden Casket. By the Author of "Little Hazel, the King's Messenger," &c. With Coloured Frontispiece and Vignette. Post 8vo, cloth extra. Price 2s. 6d.

The Crown of Glory; or, "Faithful unto Death." A Scottish Story of Martyr Times. By the Author of "Little Hazel, the King's Messenger," &c. Post 8vo, cloth extra. Price 2s. 6d.

T. NELSON AND SONS, LONDON, EDINBURGH, AND NEW YORK.

Illustrated Story-Books for the Young.

Little Snowdrop and her Golden Casket. By the Author of "Little Hazel, the King's Messenger," &c. With Coloured Frontispiece and Vignette. Post 8vo, cloth. Price 2s. 6d.

Under the Old Oaks; or, Won by Love. By the Author of "Little Hazel, the King's Messenger," &c. With Coloured Frontispiece and Vignette. Post 8vo, cloth. Price 2s. 6d.

Little Hazel, the King's Messenger. By the Author of "Little Snowdrop and her Golden Casket," &c. With Coloured Frontispiece and Vignette. Post 8vo, cloth. Price 2s. 6d.

Tinsel and Gold; or, What Girls should Learn. A Tale. By Mrs. VEITCH. Foolscap 8vo, cloth. Price 1s. 6d.

The Story of Little Robinson of Paris; or, The Triumph of Industry. Translated from the French. By LUCY LANDON. Foolscap 8vo, cloth. Price 2s.

Old Robin and his Proverb; or, With the Lowly is Wisdom. By Mrs. HENRY F. BROCK. With Coloured Frontispiece and Vignette, and Sixteen Illustrations. Royal 18mo, cloth. Price 1s.

Little Lily's Travels. With Coloured Frontispiece and Vignette, and Twenty-two Illustrations. Royal 18mo, cloth. Price 1s. 6d.

Grandpapa's Keepsakes; or, Take Heed will Surely Speed. By Mrs. GEORGE CUPPLES, Author of "The Story of Our Doll," &c. With Coloured Frontispiece and Vignette, and Forty-five Engravings. Royal 18mo, cloth. Price 1s. 6d.

The Golden Rule; or, Do to Others as you would have Others do to You. Royal 18mo, cloth. Price 1s. 6d.

Pictorial Library of Travel and Adventure.

Pictures of **Travel in Far-off** Lands. A Companion to the Study of Geography.—CENTRAL AMERICA. With Fifty Engravings. Extra foolscap, cloth. Price 2s.

Pictures of **Travel** in Far-off Lands—South America. With Fifty Engravings. Extra foolscap, cloth. Price 2s.

Doctor Kane, **the** Arctic Hero. A Narrative of his Adventures and Explorations in the Polar Regions. By M. JONES. With Coloured Frontispiece and Vignette, and Thirty-five Engravings. Foolscap 8vo. Price 2s.

Round the World. A Story of Travel Compiled from the Narrative of Ida Pfeiffer. By D. MURRAY SMITH. With Tinted Frontispiece and Vignette, and Thirty-five Engravings on Wood. Extra foolscap, cloth. Price 2s.

Afar in the Forest; or, Pictures of Life and Scenery **in the** Wilds of Canada. By Mrs. TRAILL, Author of "The Canadian Crusoes," **&c.** With Coloured Frontispiece and Vignette, and Twenty-two **Engravings.** Foolscap 8vo, cloth. Price 2s.

The Adventures of Mark Willis. By Mrs. GEORGE CUPPLES. With Coloured Frontispiece and Vignette, **and** Forty-five Engravings. Royal 18mo. Price 1s. 6d.

The **Young Crusoe;** or, A Boy's Adventures on a Desolate Island. By Mrs. HOFLAND. With Coloured Frontispiece and Vignette, and Fourteen Engravings. Foolscap 8vo, cloth extra. Price 2s. 6d.

Robert and Harold; or, The Young Marooners. A Tale of Adventure on the Coast of Florida. By F. R. GOULDING. With Six Tinted Plates. Post 8vo, cloth extra. Price 2s. 6d.

Home Amid the Snow; or, Warm Hearts in Cold Regions. By CAPTAIN CHARLES EDE, R.N. With Tinted Frontispiece and Vignette, and Twenty-eight Engravings. Foolscap 8vo, cloth. Price 2s.

Books for the Young.

RICHLY ILLUSTRATED.

Things in the Forest. By Mary and Elizabeth Kirby. With Coloured Frontispiece and Vignette, and Fifty Illustrations. Royal 18mo, cloth. Price 1s. 6d.

The Children on the Plains. A Story of Travel and Adventure in the Great Prairies of North America. By the Author of "The Babes in the Basket." With Coloured Frontispiece and Vignette, and Sixteen Illustrations. Royal 18mo, cloth. Price 1s. 6d.

Truth is Always Best; or, "A Fault Confessed is Half Redressed." By Mary and Elizabeth Kirby. With Coloured Frontispiece and Vignette, and Seventeen Illustrations. Royal 18mo, cloth. Price 1s. 6d.

The Story of Reuben Inch; or, The Power of Perseverance. By the Author of "Copsley Annals," "Village Missionaries," &c. With Coloured Frontispiece and Vignette, and Twenty Illustrations. Royal 18mo, cloth. Price 1s. 6d.

Lessons on the Life of Christ for the Little Ones at Home. By the Author of "Hymns from the Land of Luther." With Coloured Frontispiece and Vignette, and Thirty Engravings. Royal 18mo, cloth. Price 1s. 6d.

Illustrated Story-Books for the Young.

By the Author of "Copsley Annals," "Village Missionaries," &c.

Matty's Hungry Missionary-Box, and Other Stories. With Coloured Frontispiece and Vignette, and Thirty Engravings. Royal 18mo, cloth. Price 1s.

It's his Way, and Other Stories. With Coloured Frontispiece and Vignette. Royal 18mo, cloth. 1s.

The Two Watches, and Other Stories. With Coloured Frontispiece and Vignette. Royal 18mo, cloth. 1s.

Under the Microscope; or, "Thou shalt call me My Father." With Coloured Frontispiece and Vignette, and Seventeen Engravings. Royal 18mo, cloth. Price 1s. 6d.

T. NELSON AND SONS, LONDON, EDINBURGH, AND NEW YORK.

www.ingramcontent.com/pod-product-compliance
Lightning Source LLC
Chambersburg PA
CBHW032058220426
43664CB00008B/1054